Certificate in Business Accounting

Paper C05

Fundamentals of Ethics, Corporate Governance and Business Law

Assessment Kit

CIMA

KAPLAN PUBLISHING
FOULKS LYNCH

British Library Cataloguing-in-Publication Data

A catalogue record for this book is available from the British Library.

Kaplan Publishing Foulks Lynch
Unit 2
Business Centre
Molly Millars Lane
Wokingham
Berkshire RG41 2QZ

ISBN 1-84710-171-2
978-1-84710-171-6

Printed and bound in Great Britain

Acknowledgements

We are grateful to the Chartered Institute of Management Accountants, the Association of Chartered Certified Accountants and the Institute of Chartered Accountants in England and Wales for permission to reproduce past examination questions. The answers have been prepared by Kaplan Publishing Foulks Lynch.

INTRODUCTION

We have worked closely with experienced CIMA tutors and lecturers to ensure that our Kits are exam-focused and user-friendly.

This Assessment Kit includes an extensive selection of questions that entirely cover the syllabus – this ensures that your knowledge is tested across all syllabus areas. Wherever possible questions have been grouped by syllabus topics.

All questions are of exam standard and format – this enables you to master the exam techniques.

There is a mock exam at the back of the book – try it under timed conditions (two hours) and this will give you an exact idea of the way you will be tested in your exam.

CONTENTS

SYLLABUS AND LEARNING OUTCOMES

Learning aims

This syllabus aims to test the student's ability to:

- discuss the framework of professional values, ethics and attitudes for exercising professional judgement and acting in an ethical manner, which is in the best interests of society and the profession
- explain the need to comply with the CIMA and IFAC Codes of Ethics for Professional Accountants
- explain the importance of good corporate governance and the evolution of good practice
- explain fundamental aspects of the organisation and operation of the English legal system and compare and contrast it with other legal systems
- explain the elements of the tort of negligence and the manner in which the tort impacts upon professional advisers
- explain the essential elements of a simple contract, what is regarded as adequate performance of the simple contract, and the remedies available to the innocent party in the event of a breach
- explain the essential differences between sole traderships, partnerships and companies limited by shares
- explain the way in which companies are administered, financed and managed
- apply legal knowledge to solve business problems.

A Ethics and Business – 15%

Learning outcomes

On completion of their studies students should be able to:

- apply the values and attitudes that provide professional accountants with a commitment to act in the public interest and with social responsibility
- explain the need for a framework of laws, regulations and standards in business and their application
- explain the nature of ethics and its application to business and the accountancy profession
- identify the difference between detailed rules-based and framework approaches to ethics
- explain the need for continual personal improvement and lifelong learning
- explain the need to develop the virtues of reliability, responsibility, timeliness, courtesy and respect

- explain the ethical principles of integrity, objectivity, professional competence, due care and confidentiality
- identify the concepts of independence, scepticism, accountability and social responsibility
- explain the reasons why CIMA and IFAC each have a Code of Ethics for Professional Accountants.

Indicative syllabus content

- Values and attitudes for professional accountants
- Legal frameworks, regulations and standards for business
- The nature of ethics and its relevance to business and the accountancy profession
- Rules-based and framework approaches to ethics
- Personal development and lifelong learning
- Personal qualities of reliability, responsibility, timeliness, courtesy and respect
- Ethical principles of integrity, objectivity, professional competence, due care and confidentiality
- Concepts of independence, scepticism, accountability and social responsibility
- The CIMA and IFAC Codes of Ethics for Professional Accountants

B Ethical Conflict – 10%

Learning outcomes

On completion of their studies students should be able to:

- explain the relationship between ethics, governance, the law and social responsibility
- describe the consequences of unethical behaviour to the individual, the profession and society
- identify situations where ethical dilemmas and conflicts of interest occur
- explain how ethical dilemmas and conflicts of interest can be resolved.

Indicative syllabus content

- The relationship between ethics, governance, the law and social responsibility
- Unethical behaviour
- Ethical dilemmas and conflicts of interest

C Corporate Governance – 10%

Learning outcomes

On completion of their studies students should be able to:

- define corporate governance
- explain the interaction of corporate governance with business ethics and company law
- describe the history of corporate governance internationally
- explain the effects of corporate governance on directors' behaviour and their duties of skill and care
- explain different board structures, the role of the board and corporate governance issues

- describe the types of policies and procedures that 'best practice' companies introduce
- explain the regulatory governance framework for companies.

Indicative syllabus content

- The role and key objectives of corporate governance in relation to ethics and the law.
- The development of corporate governance internationally
- The behaviour of directors in relation to corporate governance and the duty of care towards their stakeholders
- The role of the board in establishing corporate governance standards
- Types of board structures and corporate governance issues
- Policies and procedures for 'best practice' companies
- Rules-based and principles-based approaches to governance
- The regulatory governance framework

D Comparison of English Law with Alternative Legal Systems – 10%

Learning outcomes

On completion of their studies students should be able to:

- explain the manner in which behaviour within society is regulated by the civil and the criminal laws
- identify and explain the sources of English law
- illustrate the operation of the doctrine of precedent by reference to the essential elements of the tort of negligence and its application to professional advisers
- compare and contrast the elements of alternative legal systems, Sharia law and the role of international legal regulations.

Indicative syllabus content

- The sources of English law
- The system of judicial precedent
- The essential elements of the tort of negligence, including duty, breach and damage/loss/injury and the liability of professionals in respect of negligent advice
- Alternative legal systems, including codified (civil law) systems, Sharia law and international legal regulations

E The Law of Contract – 20%

Learning outcomes

On completion of their studies students should be able to:

- identify the essential elements of a valid simple contract and situations where the law requires the contract to be in a particular form
- explain how the law determines whether negotiating parties have reached agreement and the role of consideration in making that agreement enforceable
- explain when the parties will be regarded as intending the agreement to be legally binding and how and agreement may be avoided because of misrepresentations

- explain how the contents and the terms of a contract are established and the possible repercussions of non-performance
- explain how the law controls the use of unfair terms in respect of both consumer and non-consumer business agreements
- explain what the law regards as performance of the contract, and valid and invalid reasons for non-performance
- explain the type of breach necessary to cause contractual breakdown and the remedies that are available for serious and minor breaches of contract.

Indicative syllabus content

- The essential elements of a valid simple contract
- The legal status of statements made by negotiating parties: enforceable offers and acceptances, and the application of the rules to standard form contracts using modern forms of communication and the role of consideration
- The principles for establishing that the parties intend their agreement to have contractual force and how a contract is affected by a misrepresentation
- Incorporation of express and implied terms, conditions and warranties
- The main provisions of sale of goods and supply of services legislation
- The manner in which the law controls the use of exclusion clauses and unfair terms in consumer and non-consumer transactions
- The level of performance sufficient to discharge contractual obligations
- Valid reasons for non performance by way of agreement, breach by the other party and frustration
- The remedies of specific performance, injunction, rescission, and requiring a contract party to pay the agreed price
- Causation and remoteness of damages, and their quantification

F The Law of Employment – 10%

Learning outcomes

On completion of their studies students should be able to:

- explain the difference between employees and independent contractors and how the contents of a contract of employment are established
- explain the distinction between unfair and wrongful dismissal
- demonstrate an awareness of how employers and employees are affected by health and safety legislation, including the consequences of a failure to comply.

Indicative syllabus content

- The tests used to distinguish an employee from an independent contractor
- The express and implied terms of a contract of employment
- Unfair and wrongful dismissal
- An outline of the main rules relating to health and safety at work, sanctions on employers for non-compliance, and remedies for employees

G Company Administration and Finance – 25%

Learning outcomes

On completion of their studies students should be able to:

- explain the essential characteristics of the different forms of business organisations and the implications of corporate personality
- explain the differences between public and private companies and establishing a company by registration or purchasing 'off the shelf'
- explain the purpose and legal status of the memorandum and articles of association
- explain the ability of a company to contract
- explain the main advantages and disadvantages of carrying on business through the medium of a company limited by shares
- explain the use and procedure of board meetings and general meetings of shareholders
- explain the voting rights of directors and shareholders and identify the various types of shareholder resolutions
- explain the nature of different types of share, the procedure for the issue of shares, and acceptable forms of payment
- explain the maintenance of capital principle and the procedure to increase and reduce share capital, including the repercussions of issuing shares for an improper purpose
- explain the ability of a company to take secured and unsecured loans, the different types of security and the registration procedure
- explain the procedure for the appointment, retirement, disqualification and removal of directors and their powers and duties during office
- explain the rules dealing with the possible imposition of personal liability upon the directors of insolvent companies
- identify and contrast the rights of shareholders with the board of a company
- explain the qualifications, powers and duties of the company secretary.

Indicative syllabus content

- The essential characteristics of sole traderships/practitionerships, partnerships, companies limited by shares and corporate personality
- 'Lifting the corporate veil' both at common law and by statute
- The distinction between public and private companies
- The procedure for registering a company, the advantages of purchasing a company 'off the shelf', and the purpose and contents of the memorandum and articles of association
- Corporate capacity to contract
- Board meetings: when used and the procedure at the meeting
- Annual and Extraordinary General Meetings: when used and the procedure at the meeting including company resolutions and the uses of each type of resolution
- The rights attaching to the different types of shares and the purposes and procedures for issuing shares

- The maintenance of capital principle, the purposes and rules for which shares may be issued, redeemed or, purchased and the provision of financial assistance for the purchase of its own shares
- The ability of a company to borrow money and the procedure to be followed
- Unsecured loans, and the nature and effect of fixed and floating charges
- The appointment, retirement and removal of directors and their powers and duties during office
- Fraudulent and wrongful trading, preferences and transactions at an under-value
- The division of powers between the board and the shareholders
- The rights of majority and minority shareholders
- The qualifications, powers and duties of the company secretary.

REVISION GUIDANCE

Planning your revision

Begin by asking yourself two questions:

how much time do I have available for revision?

Remember to take into account:

- times of the day when you work most effectively
- other commitments
- time definitely unavailable (e.g. holidays)
- relaxation time.

what do I need to cover during my revision?

Remember to take into account that:

- all syllabus areas are equally examinable
- you need more time when revising areas of the syllabus you feel least confident about
- question practice is the best form of revision.

Make a timetable/plan to remind yourself how much work you have to do and when you are free to do it. Allow some time for slippage.

Revision techniques

- Go through your notes and textbook **highlighting the important points**
- You might want to produce your own set of **summarised notes**
- **List key words** for each topic to remind you of the essential concepts
- **Practise exam-standard questions**, under timed conditions
- **Rework questions** that you got completely wrong the first time, but only when you think you know the subject better
- If you get stuck on topics, **find someone to explain** them to you (your tutor or a colleague, for example)
- **Read recent articles** on the CIMA website and in *Insider*
- **Read** good newspapers and professional journals.

COMPUTER BASED ASSESSMENT

Format of the assessment

	Number of marks
75 objective test questions	100

Total time allowed: two hours

About the assessment

- The process for entering for a Computer Based Assessment (CBA) is different from entering for a paper based exam.
- Contact CIMA or look up on the CIMA website to find out where your nearest CIMA accredited CBA centre is. Contact the centre and arrange to sit the assessment.
- With CBAs the most common type of questions is 'multiple choice', where you have to choose the correct answer from a list of possible answers, but there are a variety of other **objective question types** that can be used within the system. These include true/false questions, matching pairs of text and graphic, sequencing and ranking, labelling diagrams and single and multiple numeric entry. There are also questions that carry several marks.
- You need to be sure you **know how to answer questions** of this type before you sit the assessment. You will achieve this through practice.
- Whatever the format, these questions require that you have *learnt* definitions, *know* key words and their meanings and importance, and *understand* the names and meanings of rules, concepts and theories.
- Do not attempt a CBA until you have **completed all study material** relating to it.
- **Do not skip any of the material** in the syllabus.
- Before you start the assessment make sure you understand how to use the **software**. If in doubt, ask the assessment centre staff to explain it to you.
- With CBAs questions are **displayed on the screen** and answers are entered using keyboard and mouse.
- **Read each question** *very* carefully.
- **Double-check your answer** before committing yourself to it.
- If you are answering a multiple-choice question, eliminate first those answers that you know are definitely wrong. Then choose the most appropriate answer from those that are left.
- Remember that **only one answer to a multiple-choice question can be right**.
- Answer *every* question – if you do not know an answer, you don't lose anything by guessing. Think carefully before you **guess**.
- **Don't panic** if you realise you've answered a question incorrectly – you can always go back and change your answer.
- At the end of the assessment, you are given a **certificate showing the result** you have achieve

Section 1

OBJECTIVE TEST QUESTIONS

Each question carries two marks unless stated otherwise.

SYLLABUS SECTION A: ETHICS AND BUSINESS

1 Which of the following is not a reason why accountants must keep themselves up-to-date professionally?

A It is a requirement of the *Seven Principles of Public Life*.

B They have a duty to maintain professional knowledge and skill.

C They have a duty to provide a client or employer with competent professional service.

D It is a requirement of CIMA's *Code of Ethics for Professional Accountants*.

2 What is meant by accountability?

A Taking responsibility for your own work

B Maintaining records that provide evidence to back up your conclusions

C Being answerable to queries in relation to your work

D All of the above

3 Which of the following does not specifically relate to business ethics?

A How a business conducts its relationships with its customers

B How a company does business, rather than what it does

C The behaviour of the business and its employees

D The financial viability of a business

4 Which of the following is the key attribute required of an accountant's work?

A It is submitted on time.

B It is written in clear language.

C It meets professional standards.

D It does not require further explanation.

5 Which statement below best describes the concept of scepticism?

A Maintaining an independent mind

B Doubting the views of others

C Only accepting information as correct if it has been checked by a more senior colleague

D Seeking supporting evidence before accepting information as correct

6 What is the main reason for an accountant to follow the concept of lifelong learning?

A It helps meet the requirement of due care

B To keep up-to-date with new standards

C To minimise the risk of being sued for negligence

D To maximise their potential for promotion

7 CIMA has its own *Code of Ethics for Professional Accountants* because it:

A Provides a basis for complaints or cases under CIMA's disciplinary procedures

B Tells stakeholders what is required of them in terms of behaviour

C Tells CIMA members what is and is not legally required of them

D Provides evidence that accountants behave ethically

8 Which of the following terms tends/tend to characterise a rules-based approach to ethics?

(i) Tick-box mentality

(ii) Fear driven

(iii) Prevention

A (i) only

B (i) and (ii) only

C (i), (ii) and (iii)

D (ii) and (iii) only

9 Accountants are expected to comply with the fundamental principle of objectivity. What does this require?

A Not to use information obtained in the course of their work for their own personal advantage

B Not to do anything that may bring the profession into disrepute

C To maintain intellectual honesty and impartiality

D To ensure that work produced meets the requirements and specifications of those who requested it

10 An accountant wastes their employer's resources if they fail to demonstrate which of the following virtues?

A Timeliness

B Reliability

C Responsibility

D Courtesy

11 What was the mission of IFAC's Ethics Committee?

A To eliminate unethical behaviour by accountants

B To develop high-quality ethical standards for professional accountants around the world

C To restore confidence in the accounting profession

D To regulate national accountancy bodies

12 How can an accountant demonstrate the virtue of respect?

(i) By avoiding disagreements with colleagues

(ii) By developing constructive relationships

(iii) By recognising the rights of others

A (i) and (ii) only

B (i) and (iii) only

C (ii) and (iii) only

D (i), (ii) and (iii)

13 CIMA members should pay most attention to which one of the following when taking on new work?

A Their ability to give the work their full attention

B Ensuring the work remains confidential

C Checking that they are sufficiently qualified and experienced to take on the work

D Maintaining their independence

14 What reasons does CIMA have for developing its own ethical code?

(i) Because the IFAC code is too stringent

(ii) To reflect its status as a Chartered Institute

(iii) To provide a basis for complaints under its disciplinary code

A (i) and (ii) only

B (i) and (iii) only

C (ii) and (iii) only

D (i), (ii) and (iii)

15 Independence has two key attributes. These are independence:

A Of mind and of belief

B Of belief and in appearance

C Of mind and in appearance

D None of the above

16 Which one of the following actions demonstrates independence?

A Questioning information

B Putting all irrelevant considerations to one side

C Accepting sole responsibility for your actions

D Taking a course of action that upholds the public interest

17 What does the ethical principle of integrity require?

A An accountant should be honest in all their professional dealings.

B An accountant should safeguard the security of all information in their possession.

C An accountant should maintain an unbiased state of mind.

D An accountant should avoid conflicts of interest.

18 How can an accountant demonstrate the ethical principle of due care?

A By taking all reasonable measures to safeguard the security of information

B By giving work the level of attention it deserves

C By maintaining an independent mind

D By ensuring they stay technically up-to-date

19 You are reviewing the work of a junior colleague and have discovered some serious mistakes. It is clear that he lacks the understanding of financial matters that he requires to be a competent accountant. Which of CIMA's fundamental principles does this violate?

A Professional competence and due care

B Objectivity

C Integrity

D Confidentiality

20 Accountants need to act in the public interest and with social responsibility. Which of the following would not help them to do this?

A Acting with integrity

B Defining long-term career objectives

C Abiding by the CIMA *Code of Ethics for Professional Accountants*

D Staying up-to-date with developments in business and accounting

21 Which of the following is incorrect?

A The IFAC *Code of Ethics* takes a rules-based approach.

B The CIMA *Code of Ethics* takes a framework-based approach.

C Company codes of ethics can take a framework-based or a rules-based approach.

D Codes of ethics are often based on core values or principles.

22 Which one of the following is not a fundamental principle in CIMA's *Code of Ethics*?

A Professional competence

B Reliability

C Objectivity

D Integrity

23 Which one of the five fundamental principles requires an accountant to avoid action that discredits the profession?

A Objectivity

B Integrity

C Confidentiality

D Professional behaviour

24 Which one of the following statements concerning the disclosure of confidential information is incorrect?

A An accountant can disclose confidential information to public authorities when infringements of the law come to light.

B An accountant can disclose confidential information in the course of legal proceedings.

C An accountant can disclose confidential information to comply with the quality review of a professional body.

D An accountant must never disclose confidential information unless authorised by the client.

25 Which of the following is not one of the fundamental principles set out in CIMA's *Code of Ethics*?

A Confidentiality

B Objectivity

C Accountability

D Integrity

26 Which one of the following is not one of the *Seven Principles of Public Life* issued by the Committee on Standards in Public Life?

A Selflessness

B Objectivity

C Accountability

D Confidentiality

27 Which of the following terms tends/tend to characterise a framework-based approach to ethics?

(i) Implicit

(ii) Values driven

(iii) Detection

A (i) only

B (i) and (ii) only

C (i), (ii) and (iii)

D (ii) and (iii) only

28 Which of the following statements is incorrect?

A If you omit information or make false or misleading statements, you are failing to comply with the fundamental principle of professional competence and due care.

B If you allow bias or a conflict of interest to override your professional judgment, you are failing to comply with the fundamental principle of objectivity.

C If you use information acquired as a result of business relationships for your own personal advantage, you are failing to comply with the fundamental principle of confidentiality.

D If you bring your profession into disrepute, you are failing to comply with the fundamental principle of professional behaviour.

29 Which one of the following statements concerning confidentiality is incorrect?

A An accountant is required to disclose confidential information to public authorities when infringements of the law come to light.

B An accountant is permitted to produce confidential information in the course of legal proceedings if the client authorises the disclosure.

C An accountant may use prior experience but not prior information gained in a previous role.

D Confidentiality extends after the end of the relationship with the client or employer.

30 Which of the following lists consists wholly of fundamental principles from CIMA's *Code of Ethics*?

A Professional behaviour, confidentiality, objectivity, courtesy

B Professional competence and due care, integrity, reliability

C Confidentiality, integrity, honesty, professional behaviour

D Objectivity, integrity, professional competence and due care

31 Which of the following lists does not consist wholly of personal qualities and virtues sought by CIMA?

A Courtesy, responsibility, reliability and respect

B Respect, reliability, responsibility and timeliness

C Timeliness, courtesy, honesty and respect

D Responsibility, respect, courtesy and timeliness

32 Which of the following statements demonstrate that an accountant is complying with the fundamental principle of professional behaviour?

(i) Acting diligently in accordance with applicable technical and professional standards

(ii) Not making exaggerated claims for the services they are able to offer or the experience they have gained

(iii) Not making disparaging references or unsubstantiated comparisons to the work of others

A (i), (ii) and (iii)

B (i) and (ii)

C (ii) and (iii)

D (i) and (iii)

33 Which of the following terms tends/tend to characterise a framework-based approach to ethics?

(i) Spirit of the law

(ii) Discretionary

(iii) Difficult to measure

A (i) only

B (i) and (ii) only

C (i), (ii) and (iii)

D (ii) and (iii) only

34 Independence in appearance requires which of the following?

(i) Expressing a conclusion without being affected by influences that compromise professional judgment

(ii) Allowing an individual to exercise objectivity and professional scepticism

(iii) Avoiding facts and circumstances that are so significant that a reasonable and informed third party would conclude that an individual's objectivity had been compromised

A (i), (ii) and (iii)

B (i) and (ii) only

C (i) and (iii) only

D (iii) only

SYLLABUS SECTION B: ETHICAL CONFLICT

35 Which of the following is incorrect?

A CIMA's members must adhere to the IFAC *Code of Ethics*.

B Ethical guidelines and standards encourage good practice.

C Accountants are required by law to follow ethical guidelines and standards.

D CIMA's members must adhere to CIMA's *Code of Ethics*.

36 Which of the following are possible consequences to the accounting profession if unethical behaviour is widespread?

(i) The introduction of legislation

(ii) Loss of its reputation

(iii) Loss of its chartered institute status

A (i) and (ii) only

B (ii) and (iii) only

C (i) and (iii) only

D (i), (ii) and (iii)

37 Which of the following is/are not a consequence to society of accountants behaving unethically?

(i) Inefficient stock markets

(ii) Inappropriate investment decisions by businesses

(iii) Loss of confidence in financial reports

A (i) and (ii) only

B (ii) and (iii) only

C (i) and (iii) only

D (i), (ii) and (iii)

38 Which of the following are possible consequences to a CIMA member following their unethical behaviour?

(i) Disciplinary action by CIMA

(ii) Loss of employment

(iii) Feelings of shame

(iv) Loss of reputation

A (i) and (ii) only

B (i), (ii) and (iii) only

C (i), (ii) and (iv) only

D All of the above

39 An old friend has asked you to tender for accounting work. You are keen to assist. From an ethical as well as a business perspective, what is the most appropriate action for you to take?

A Tender for the work.

B Suggest to your friend that they approach more than one company to create a competitive tender.

C Suggest to your friend that they assign the work to a different company instead.

D Ask a colleague to handle the client.

40 You have recently begun a relationship with a member of another department. You are a password holder for that other department's computer system. From an ethical perspective, what is the most appropriate action for you to take?

A Suggest to your manager that new password system controls are introduced, but without explaining why.

B Tell your manager about the relationship.

C No action is required as the relationship might not last.

D End the relationship.

41 Just prior to your company's external audit, your manager suggests that you offer to take the auditors to Cheltenham to see the racing. From an ethical perspective, what is the most appropriate action for you to take?

A Query the suggestion with your manager.

B Do as your manager suggests.

C Refuse to do as your manager suggests.

D Claim you are too busy.

42 You have recently been promoted to the position of deputy accountant to the Finance Director. You are delighted with the promotion, but within a few weeks of starting your new role you realise you lack sufficient expertise to take on this responsibility. From an ethical perspective, that is the most appropriate action for you to take?

A Undertake some additional training in your spare time.

B Talk to your manager about the situation.

C Seek another job before your lack of expertise is discovered.

D Keep quiet in the hope you will get to grips with the role before you are found out.

43 Delia's boss has asked her to book a proportion of future sales into this year's accounts. She has been told that the paperwork will follow by the year end and that the factory is about to begin to make the products required.

What should Delia do?

A Do as requested.

B Refuse to carry out the request.

C Ask for the request in writing.

D Challenge the request.

44 Which of the following is not an example of a self-review threat?

A The long association of a senior member of the assurance team with the assurance client

B A member of the assurance team being, or having recently been, a director or officer of that client

C Reporting on the operation of a financial system after being involved in its design or implementation

D Having prepared the original data used to generate records that are the subject matter of the engagement

45 A threat that may occur as a result of the financial or other interests of a close family member of an accountant is known as which of the following?

A A self-interest threat

B An advocacy threat

C A familiarity threat

D A self-review threat

46 Which of the following is not an example of an engagement-specific safeguard in the workplace?

A Discussing ethical issues with those charged with governance of the client

B Leadership that stresses the importance of compliance with the fundamental principles

C Involving another company to perform or re-perform the work done

D Consulting an independent third party

47 Which of the following statements is incorrect?

A An intimidation threat may occur when an accountant is deterred from acting objectively by threats, actual or perceived.

B An advocacy threat may occur when an accountant promotes an opinion to the point that subsequent objectivity may be compromised.

C A self-review threat may occur when a previous judgment needs to be re-evaluated by the accountant responsible for that judgement.

D A self-interest threat may occur when, because of a close relationship, an accountant becomes too sympathetic to the interests of others.

48 Which of the following is not an example of a self-interest threat?

A A loan to or from an assurance client or any of its directors of officers

B Concern about the possibility of losing a client

C Being threatened with litigation

D Potential employment with a client

49 Which of the following is not an example of a familiarity threat?

A Accepting gifts or preferential treatment from a client

B Having a close business relationship with a client

C Having a close family relationship with a director of a client

D A former partner of the company being a director of the client

50 A client wishes to entrust you with a large sum of cash. Which of the following options describes the appropriate course of action you should take?

A Refuse to accept the cash.

B Pay the cash into the company's business bank account.

C Pay the cash into your personal bank account.

D Pay the cash into a separate bank account kept specifically for client money.

51 Which of the following circumstances may create a self-interest threat for a professional accountant in business?

(i) Commercial pressure from outside the employing organisation

(ii) Concern over employment security

(iii) Long association with business contacts influencing business decisions

A (i) and (ii) only

B (i) and (iii) only

C (ii) and (iii)

D (i), (ii), and (iii)

52 Which of the following circumstances may create an intimidation threat for a professional accountant in business?

(i) Threat of dismissal or replacement over a disagreement about the way financial information is to be reported

(ii) A dominant personality attempting to influence the decision making process

(iii) An accountant in a position to influence financial reporting having a close family member who is in a position to benefit from that influence

A (i) and (ii) only

B (i) and (iii) only

C (ii) and (iii)

D (i), (ii), and (iii)

53 You are eligible for a profit-related bonus. The value of that bonus could be directly affected by the decisions you make in your job. These circumstances are an example of which type of threat?

A Familiarity

B Intimidation

C Self-review

D Self-interest

54 Which of the following would be a useful test for resolving an ethical dilemma?

(i) Imagining how you would feel if your decision was reported in the local press

(ii) Imagining whether your decision would make you more popular in the office

(iii) Imagining how your family would react to your decision

A (i) and (ii) only

B (i) and (iii) only

C (ii) and (iii)

D (i), (ii), and (iii)

55 Which of the following would not help you find an answer to an ethical dilemma?

(i) Referring to the CIMA *Code of Ethics*

(ii) Establishing the facts and the ethical issues involved

(iii) Ignoring the issue on the basis that it will resolve itself in time

A (i) only

B (i) and (ii) only

C (iii) only

D (ii) and (iii) only

56 One of your colleagues makes his employees' lives a misery. He constantly criticises them, makes unreasonable demands and threatens to fire them if their work contains errors.

The least likely consequence for your colleague is:

A A severe reprimand

B Investigation by the company's internal complaints team

C Dismissal

D Praise from his line manager for getting the best from his staff

57 Which of the following is not an example of a company-wide safeguard in the work environment?

A Policies to enable the identification of interests or relationships between the company and clients

B Designating a senior member of staff to be responsible for overseeing the functioning of the company's quality control system

C Disclosing to those charged with governance of the client the nature of services provided and extent of fees charged

D Leadership of the company that establishes the expectation that staff will act in the public interest

SYLLABUS SECTION C: CORPORATE GOVERNANCE

58 Which one of the following is not a recommendation of the Cadbury Committee?

A The appointment of an audit committee consisting of a majority of non-executive directors

B Independent non-executive directors to be appointed to the boards of listed companies

C The imposition of a three-year maximum term on non-executive directors' service contracts, unless approved by the shareholders

D Non-executive directors to set the remuneration of executive directors

59 The Sarbanes-Oxley Act applies to which of the following?

A All publicly traded companies listed in the United States

B United States companies listed in the United States

C All United States companies

D Foreign companies listed in the United States

60 Which of the following reports did not form the basis of the Combined Code when it was originally issued?

A The Hampel Report

B The Greenbury Report

C The Turnbull Report

C The Cadbury Report

61 Which one of the following options correctly states the number of independent non-executive directors required by the Combined Code?

A FTSE 350 listed companies require half their board to be independent non-executive directors.

B FTSE 350 listed companies require two-thirds of their board to be independent non-executive directors.

C All companies require half their board to be independent non-executive directors.

D Small listed companies require at least three independent non-executive directors.

62 Which of the following individuals could be regarded as being independent?

(i) A person who has been an employee of the company in the previous five years

(ii) A person who has had a material business relationship with the company in the previous three years

(iii) A person who has served on the board of the company for more than nine years

A (i) only

B (ii) only

C (iii) only

D None of them

63 Corporate governance is primarily for the benefit of stakeholders. What are stakeholders in this context?

A The shareholders

B All those indirectly affected by the company's activities

C All those directly affected by the company's activities

D All those directly or indirectly affected by the company's activities

64 Which one of the following is correct?

A A listed public company has complied with the Combined Code if it produces a report explaining why it has not complied with its recommendations.

B It is a criminal offence for a listed company to fail to comply with the Combined Code

C A public company may be sued for breach of statutory duty if it fails to comply with the Combined Code.

D The Combined Code has no status and may be ignored by all companies

65 To which of the following does a director owe a duty of care and skill?

(i) The public at large

(ii) The company's creditors

(iii) The shareholders

A (i) only

B (i) and (iii) only

C (ii) only

D (iii) only

66 Which of the following are not represented at board level in the United Kingdom?

(i) Creditors

(ii) Shareholders

(iii) Employees

A (i) and (iii) only

B (iii) only

C (i) and (ii) only

D (i) only

67 Which one of the following is correct in relation to the Combined Code?

A A failure to comply with the Combined Code may result in a finding of wrongful trading on the part of the directors.

B Acting in ignorance of the Combined Code may result in a director being disqualified from acting as a director.

C The Combined Code requires disclosure of the extent to which it has been complied with.

D The Combined Code gives rise to civil but not criminal liability.

68 Which of the following are examples of unitary board structures?

(i) An all-executive board

(ii) A majority executive board

(iii) A majority non-executive board

A (i) only

B (i) and (ii) only

C (i), (ii) and (iii)

D (ii) and (iii) only

69 Which of the following types of committee is not recommended by the Combined Code?

A Audit committee

B Nominations committee

C Remuneration committee

D Planning committee

70 Which one of the following statements was not a recommendation of the Greenbury Committee?

A Directors should never be given discounted share options.

B Annual bonuses should be pensionable.

C The remuneration committee should consider the interests of both the shareholders and the directors when determining the level of directors' remuneration.

D Any long-term incentive schemes to be offered to directors should first be approved by the shareholders.

71 Which of the following is correct?

(i) Procedures for board meetings will be set out in the company's Articles of Association.

(ii) Procedures for board meetings must be set out in the company's Memorandum of Association.

(iii) Usually at board meetings directors have one vote each, a matter is decided upon by simple majority, and the chairman has a casting vote.

A (i) only

B (ii) only

C (ii) and (iii) only

D (i) and (iii) only

72 Which of the following committees was primarily concerned with directors' remuneration?

A Cadbury Committee

B Greenbury Committee

C Hampel Committee

D Turnbull Committee

73 D is a director of XYZ Ltd and is in breach of his duty of care and skill. Which of the following, as a general rule, is entitled to initiate action against him?

(i) The majority shareholders of XYZ Ltd

(ii) All the shareholders of XYZ Ltd

(iii) XYZ Ltd

A (i) only

B (ii) only

C (iii) only

D (i), (ii) and (iii)

74 Which one of the following statements was not a recommendation of the Hampel Committee?

A Directors' service contracts should not exceed 12 months.

B Directors should be obliged to seek re-election every three years.

C All companies should have a nomination committee for recommending new board appointments.

D The remuneration of executive directors should be based upon the recommendations of a remuneration committee comprised mainly of non-executive directors.

75 Which of the following statements is incorrect?

A Directors owe a common law duty of care to the shareholders as a body.

B The directors' common law duty of care is enforceable by the company.

C The rules and standards that make up corporate governance are aimed at the company's stakeholders.

D The stakeholders can enforce the rules of corporate governance.

76 To which type of company is the Combined Code primarily directed?

A All listed companies

B All private companies

C All public companies

D All companies

77 The two-tier board structure comprises a management board and what other type of board?

A A board of non-executive directors

B An all-executive board

C A board representing the employees

D A supervisory board

78 Which of the following statements are correct?

(i) The primary function of non-executive directors is to give an independent judgment on issues of strategy.

(ii) The chief executive is responsible for leadership of the board and setting its agenda.

(iii) A senior independent director should be made available as a contact for shareholders.

A (i) and (ii) only

B (ii) and (iii) only

C (i), (ii) and (iii)

D (i) and (iii) only

79 Which of the following statements concerning directors' duties are correct?

(i) A director must exhibit the degree of skill that could be expected of a reasonably diligent person having the general knowledge, skill and experience that they have.

(ii) A director is not bound to give their continuous attention to the affairs of the company.

(iii) In the absence of suspicious circumstances, a director is justified in trusting the company's management to perform their responsibilities in an honest manner.

A (i) and (ii)

B (ii) and (iii)

C (i) and (iii)

D (i), (ii) and (iii)

80 Which of the following statements is incorrect?

A The Turnbull Report was concerned with evaluating risks and ensuring that effective controls were put in place to reduce them.

B The Higgs Report emphasised collective board responsibility.

C Many of the Higgs Report's proposals were incorporated into the Revised Combined Code.

D The Smith Report dealt with the role and responsibilities of nominations committees.

SYLLABUS SECTION D: COMPARISON OF ENGLISH LAW WITH ALTERNATIVE LEGAL SYSTEMS

81 Appeals from the County Court are normally directed to the:

A High Court

B Court of Appeal

C European Court of Justice

D Crown Court

82 The principal objective of the criminal law is:

A To punish offenders

B To regulate behaviour within society

C To provide a remedy for the victims of crime

D To compensate the victims of crime

83 Which of the following constitutes civil proceedings?

A A prosecution for breach of health and safety legislation

B An action by a buyer claiming £3m damages from a defendant seller for mis-describing the goods offered for sale

C Proceedings where the accused is tried for the offence of applying a false trade description to goods

D A prosecution by HM Revenue & Customs for non-payment of tax

84 Which of the following is the highest court in England?

A The Crown Court

B The House of Lords

C The Queens Bench Division

D The Court of Appeal

85 Which of the following statements concerning common law and equity is/are incorrect?

(i) Equitable rights and remedies are given at the discretion of the court.

(ii) Common law prevails over equity.

(iii) An Act of Parliament can overrule any common law or equitable rule.

A (i) only

B (ii) only

C (iii) only

D (ii) and (iii) only

86 Which of the following is/are correct?

(i) In England, Parliament can delegate law-making powers to a Minister in charge of a Government department.

(ii) In England, Parliament can delegate law-making powers to professional bodies.

(iii) In England, Parliament can delegate law-making powers to local authorities.

A (iii) only

B (ii) and (iii) only

C (i) and (iii) only

D (i), (ii) and (iii)

87 Which of the following is the superior source of law?

A *Obiter dicta* of the House of Lords

B *Ratio decidendi* of the Court of Appeal

C *Obiter dicta* of the High Court

D *Ratio decidendi* of the High Court

88 Which of the following is the superior source of law?

A *Ratio decidendi* of the House of Lords

B A preliminary ruling of the European Court of Justice

C An Act of Parliament

D A bye-law

89 Which of the following statements concerning European Union directives is/are incorrect?

(i) Directives automatically have the force of law in all member states.

(ii) Directives are binding on all member states.

(iii) Directives are made by the European Parliament.

A (i) only

B (ii) only

C (i) and (iii) only

D (i), (ii) and (iii)

90 Which of the following becomes part of English law automatically?

A European Union regulations

B European Union directives

C Decisions of the Council of Ministers

D Resolutions of the European Parliament

91 Which of the following is not an essential element of the tort of negligence?

A The existence of a duty of care

B Breach of the duty of care

C An intention to cause loss

D Loss caused by the breach

92 Which of the following is/are an essential element of the tort of negligence?

(i) The existence of a duty of care

(ii) Breach of a duty of care

(iii) An intention to cause loss

A (i) and (ii) only

B (ii) and (iii) only

C (i) and (iii) only

D (i), (ii) and (iii)

93 Alan gave accountancy advice to ABC plc. ABC plc is now suing Alan in the tort of negligence to recover compensation for financial loss. ABC plc has proved that Alan owed and breached a duty of care. ABC plc can recover compensation for:

A All financial loss caused by Alan's advice

B All foreseeable financial loss caused by Alan's advice

C All reasonably foreseeable financial loss caused by Alan's advice

D All financial loss that is a direct consequence of Alan's advice

94 Anne was appointed to be the auditor of Company plc by its shareholders in a general meeting. Anne negligently certified the annual accounts as giving a true and fair view of Company plc's financial affairs. Who, as a general rule, will be able to sue Anne in the tort of negligence?

(i) Company plc's shareholders

(ii) Company plc

(iii) Company plc's directors

A (i) only

B (ii) only

C (iii) only

D (i) and (ii) only

95 In relation to the tort of negligence, which of the following is incorrect?

A A person who freely consents to run the risk of suffering harm cannot recover compensation in tort if harm is actually caused.

B *Volenti non fit injuria* is a defence.

C Contributory negligence is not a defence.

D Contributory negligence by the claimant causes an award of damages against a defendant to be reduced.

96 In relation to the tort of negligence, which of the following is incorrect?

A *Res ipsa loquitur* means 'the thing speaks for itself'.

B The effect of a successful plea of *res ipsa loquitur* is to reverse the burden of proof of negligence.

C *Res ipsa loquitur* is a defence to an action in negligence.

D A claimant can only plead *res ipsa loquitur* if the thing that caused the harm is under the control of the defendant.

97 In the tort of negligence, damages are payable in respect of:

A Reasonably foreseeable losses

B Losses that are a direct consequence of the breach of duty

C All the losses caused by the breach of duty

D Losses that are within the contemplation of the parties

98 In *Caparo Industries plc v Dickman* (1991) the House of Lords decided not to follow the precedents set in previous House of Lords decisions. They decided this on the basis that the facts of the previous cases were different from the situation in *Caparo*. Which of the following terms describes the action taken by House of Lords?

A Reversing

B Disapproving

C Distinguishing

D Overruling

99 What was the *ratio decidendi* in the case of *Donoghue v Stevenson*?

A A manufacturer owes a duty of care to those who they should reasonably foresee might be physically injured by their products.

B A claimant who only suffers financial loss cannot recover damages for negligence.

C A manufacturer of drinks must not deliberately put a snail in the bottle.

D Everyone must be nice to their neighbours.

100 Which of the following is not one of the Five Pillars of Islam?

A Obligatory

B Permissible

C Forbidden

D Tolerated

101 The European Union currently consists of how many states?

A 20

B 24

C 25

D 27

102 Which international body has the power to prosecute individuals when their own country fails to?

A European Court of Justice

B International Court of Justice

C International Criminal Court

D The United Nations

SYLLABUS SECTION E: THE LAW OF CONTRACT

103 Which of the following is/are correct?

(i) A contract of guarantee is unenforceable unless it is evidenced in writing.

(ii) A contract made by a company must be in writing.

(iii) A contract of employment must be in writing.

A (i) only

B (i) and (iii) only

C (ii) and (iii) only

D (i), (ii) and (iii)

104 Peter and Paul have agreed to combine their businesses and, in pursuance of this, they have set up in partnership together and they have:

(i) Made a partnership agreement.

(ii) Agreed with Mary that she will be employed by the company as office manager.

(iii) Agreed with Landsell plc that the company will purchase a suite of offices from it.

Which of their agreements must be in writing in order to have contractual effect?

A (i) only

B (iii) only

C (i) and (iii) only

D (i), (ii) and (iii)

105 Which of the following is incorrect?

A If an agreement is of a social nature, it is presumed that the parties do not intend legal relations.

B If an agreement is of a business nature, the parties are presumed to have intended that it should be legally enforceable.

C If an agreement is stated to be 'binding in honour only', the parties have decided that the agreement should not have contractual force.

D If an agreement is in writing, the parties are presumed to have intended that it should be legally enforceable.

106 Office Supplies Ltd placed the following advertisement in a local newspaper: 'Special offer! We are able to offer for sale of number of 3.1m pixel top-of-the-range digital cameras at a specially reduced price of £25.90. Order now while stocks last.'

The advertisement contained a mistake in that the cameras should have been priced at £259.00. B plc immediately placed an order for 50 cameras.

Which of the following is correct?

A Office Supplies Ltd can refuse to supply B plc as the advertisement is not an offer, but an invitation to treat.

B As B plc has not yet paid for the cameras, it has no contractual right to them.

C Office Supplies Ltd can only refuse to sell the cameras to B plc if it has sold all its stock.

D B plc has accepted an offer and is contractually entitled to the 50 cameras.

107 S wrote to B offering to sell certain garden plants for £50,000. B sent a written reply asking if payment could be made by instalments. What is the legal effect of B's reply?

A B has made a counter offer.

B B has accepted A's offer.

C B has requested further information.

D B has rejected the offer.

108 ABC (printers) Ltd wrote to Bill offering him the job of servicing their printing machines and requiring acceptance of the offer by fax.

Which of the following is correct?

A The contract is concluded as soon as the faxed acceptance is sent by Bill.

B The contract is concluded as soon as the faxed acceptance is received by ABC (printers) Ltd.

C The contract cannot be concluded by fax.

D Acceptance by fax is subject to the 'post rules'.

109 Which of the following is/are correct?

(i) The postal rule can apply to the revocation of an offer.

(ii) A counter-offer terminates an offer and puts another in its place.

(iii) As a general rule the acceptance of an offer is only effective when it has been communicated to the offeror.

A (i) only

B (ii) only

C (ii) and (iii) only

D (i), (ii) and (iii)

110 Which of the following statements relating to consideration is/are incorrect?

(i) A promise to perform an existing statutory duty is sufficient to amount to good consideration.

(ii) A peppercorn is sufficient to amount to good consideration.

(iii) Past consideration is sufficient to amount to good consideration.

A (i) only

B (ii) and (iii) only

C (i) and (iii) only

D (i), (ii) and (iii)

111 On Saturday X and Y made a contract for the sale of X's car to Y. It was agreed that Y would have immediate delivery but that he need not pay the price until the end of the month.

Which of the following is correct?

A The consideration given by Y is executory consideration.

B If Y fails to pay the price at the end of the month, the contract is voidable.

C The consideration given by Y is insufficient to amount to good consideration because it is past.

D If Y fails to pay the price at the end of the month, the contract is void.

112 Which of the following statements regarding the law of misrepresentation is/are correct?

(i) Generally silence cannot amount to a misrepresentation.

(ii) All types of misrepresentation enable the innocent party to apply for rescission.

(iii) A person cannot be liable for an untrue statement where the other party could have checked whether it was true or not through inspection of readily available information.

A (i) only

B (ii) only

C (i) and (ii) only

D (i), (ii) and (iii)

113 A plc has been induced to enter into a contract by the fraudulent misrepresentation of B.

Which of the following is incorrect?

A A plc may be able to rescind the contract.

B A plc may be able to claim damages and to rescind the contract.

C A plc is entitled either to rescind the contract or to claim damages.

D A plc is entitled to refuse to perform the contract if it is still executory.

114 Which of the following is/are correct?

(i) Legal title cannot pass on a contract induced by misrepresentation.

(ii) Misrepresentation renders a contract voidable.

(iii) A misrepresentee will be denied rescission if they have acted unfairly.

A (i) only

B (ii) only

C (ii) and (iii) only

D (i), (ii) and (iii)

115 Tara was induced to enter into a contract by the innocent misrepresentation of Sam. Tara seeks rescission of the contract and damages.

Which of the following is correct?

A Rescission is a court order requiring a contract to be correctly carried out.

B Tara is entitled to rescission.

C Tara is entitled to damages.

D Rescission may be refused if Tara has acted inequitably.

116 Which of the following is/are correct?

(i) A term may be implied into a contract by a court on the ground that the term is customary in the parties' trade.

(ii) A term may be implied into a contract by a court on the ground of business efficacy.

(iii) A term may be implied into a contract by a court on the ground that it would make the contract fairer.

A (i) only

B (i) and (ii) only

C (ii) and (iii) only

D (i), (ii) and (iii)

117 Which of the following is/are correct?

(i) If a warranty is breached, the innocent party can terminate the contract.

(ii) If a condition is breached, the innocent party can terminate the contract.

(iii) If a condition is breached, the innocent party cannot claim damages unless they terminate the contract.

A (i) only

B (ii) only

C (ii) and (iii) only

D (i), (ii) and (iii)

118 PQR Ltd has contracted with STU Ltd. If PQR Ltd acts in breach of a condition, which of the following is/are correct?

(i) STU Ltd may terminate the contract and sue for damages.

(ii) STU Ltd may sue for damages but may not terminate the contract.

(iii) STU Ltd may ignore the breach and continue with the contract.

A (i) only

B (i) and (iii) only

C (ii) and (iii) only

D (i), (ii) and (iii)

119 Which of the following is/are correct?

(i) A breach of a condition entitles an innocent party to repudiate a contract unless they have affirmed the contract.

(ii) A breach of a condition entitles an innocent party to repudiate a contract whether or not they have affirmed the contract.

(iii) A breach of a condition entitles an innocent party to claim damages whether or not they have affirmed the contract.

A (i) only

B (i) and (iii) only

C (ii) and (iii) only

D (i), (ii) and (iii)

120 Buyer bought a pair of underpants from Retailer Ltd. Unknown to both Buyer and Retailer Ltd there were unsafe chemical residues in the underpants and when Buyer wore them they suffered a nasty rash. Buyer now wishes to sue Retailer Ltd for damages for breach of contract.

Which of the following is correct?

A Buyer will succeed because the underpants were not of satisfactory quality.

B Buyer will not succeed because Retailer Ltd did not know that the underpants were not of satisfactory quality.

C Buyer will succeed only if they can prove that Retailer Ltd was negligent.

D Buyer will succeed only if they can prove that it was Retailer Ltd's fault that the underpants were not of satisfactory quality.

121 Which of the following is/are incorrect?

(i) An exemption clause is always void unless it is in a signed contract.

(ii) An exemption clause is always void unless it is in writing.

(iii) An exemption clause is always void unless the contracting parties have equal bargaining power.

A (i) only

B (ii) only

C (iii) only

D (i), (ii) and (iii)

122 In a contract for the sale of goods by a business to a consumer, any attempt to exclude the term implied by the Sale of Goods Act 1979 that goods sold in the course of a business must be of satisfactory quality is:

A Void

B Void unless reasonable

C Voidable at the option of the consumer

D Valid if the consumer has signed the contract

123 Flowerpower Ltd bought 150 packets of flower seeds, for use in its nursery, from Seed Supplies plc. The contract negotiated between the two companies described the seeds as having been developed to 'produce a new type of charming blue flowers not yet available to the general public'. The contract also excluded liability for breach of all terms whether express or implied by the Sale of Goods Act 1979. When the seeds grew up, Flowerpower Ltd discovered that the flowers were the usual yellow.

Which of the following is correct?

A The exemption clause is void unless Seed Supplies plc proves that it is reasonable.

B The exemption clause is valid unless Flowerpower Ltd proves that it is unreasonable.

C The exemption clause is voidable at Flowerpower Ltd's option.

124 The Unfair Contract Terms Act 1977 provides that an attempt by any person to exclude or restrict their liability for death or personal injury resulting from negligence is:

A Void unless reasonable

B Effective only in a non-consumer transaction

C Void

D Valid

125 Which of the following is correct in relation to the Unfair Terms in Consumer Contracts Regulations 1999?

A The Regulations can only apply to consumer contracts where the terms have not been individually pre-negotiated.

B The Regulations apply to all consumer contracts.

C The Regulations state that all contracts to which it applies are void.

D The Regulations state that all exemption clauses in contracts to which it applies are void.

126 Decor Ltd contracted to fit out a shop for Suremarket plc, with the shop to be ready for use by a set date. Due to Decor Ltd's lack of adherence to safety requirements, the Health and Safety Executive have issued a notice prohibiting further work on the site until safety measures as per its improvement notice are implemented by Decor Ltd.

Which of the following gives the correct position?

A Decor Ltd can increase the contract price to cover the costs of implementing the safety measures.

B Decor Ltd will be in breach of contract if it fails to complete the fitting out by the set date.

C If Decor Ltd fails to complete the fitting out by the set date it will not be in breach of contract provided it can show that it has taken all reasonable steps to do so.

D The contract between Decor Ltd and Suremarket plc is frustrated if the actions of the Health and Safety Executive mean that it is impossible to complete the fitting out by the set date.

127 IT Ltd was under contract to install an integrated computer system in all ten of Distributor plc's premises for a price of £1m. After completing the installation in nine of the premises, IT Ltd abandoned the project because its financial problems prevented it from purchasing further materials.

Which of the following is correct?

A IT Ltd is entitled to nothing.

B IT Ltd has substantially performed the contract and is entitled to a reasonable sum in respect of the work done.

C IT Ltd has completed 90% of the work and is, therefore, entitled to £900,000.

D The contract between IT Ltd and Distributor plc is frustrated.

128 A contract is frustrated if, through no fault of the parties, it:

A Becomes impossible to perform

B Becomes more expensive to perform

C Becomes more difficult to perform

D Was impossible to perform at the time it was made

129 Zed plc contracted to hire a hotel for its annual general meeting. If the hotel becomes unavailable on the date, which of the following would provide the hotel owner with a lawful excuse for non-performance of the contract?

(i) The hotel is double-booked.

(ii) The hotel is struck by lightning and burns down.

(iii) The authorities order the closure of the hotel because of non-compliance with safety regulations.

A (i) only

B (ii) only

C (iii) only

D (ii) and (iii) only

130 Which of the following is not a remedy for breach of contract?

A Damages

B A decree of specific performance

C Action for the price

D A fine

131 Which of the following is/are correct?

(i) Damages are a common law remedy for breach of contract.

(ii) Specific performance is a common law remedy for breach of contract.

(iii) Injunction is an equitable remedy for breach of contract.

A (i) only

B (ii) and (iii) only

C (i) and (iii) only

D (i), (ii) and (iii)

132 In the event of a breach of contract, what is the purpose of damages?

(i) To ensure that the contract breaker does not profit from their breach

(ii) To punish the contract breaker

(iii) To put the innocent party in the same position they would have been in had the contract been properly performed

A (i) only

B (ii) only

C (iii) only

D (i) and (iii) only

133 Which of the following statements in relation to damages for breach of contract is/are correct?

(i) Damages are not normally awarded for personal injury.

(ii) Damages are not normally awarded for loss of profits.

(iii) Damages are not normally awarded for loss of enjoyment and distress.

A (i) only

B (ii) only

C (iii) only

D (ii) and (iii) only

134 In an action for breach of contract, the court will not award:

A Unliquidated damages

B Nominal damages

C Liquidated damages

D Punitive damages

135 In an action for a breach of contract, the damages awarded by the court may be described as:

(i) Substantial

(ii) Nominal

(iii) Liquidated

A (ii) and (iii) only

B (i) and (iii) only

C (i) and (ii) only

D (i), (ii) and (iii)

136 Which of the following is/are correct?

(i) A liquidated damages clause will be void if it amounts to a penalty clause.

(ii) A liquidated damages clause will be valid where it is a genuine attempt to pre-estimate the loss caused by a breach of contract.

(iii) A liquidated damages clause can be valid even if it is for an amount in excess of the actual loss caused by the breach of contract.

A (i) only

B (ii) only

C (i) and (ii) only

D (i), (ii) and (iii)

137 Which of the following statements about the assessment of unliquidated damages for breach of contract is incorrect?

A The measure of damages is to put the innocent party in the same position that they would have been in had the contract been properly performed.

B The damages may be substantial or nominal.

C Under the rule in *Hadley v Baxendale*, damages are always recoverable for normal loss.

D Under the rule in *Hadley v Baxendale*, damages are not recoverable for abnormal loss.

138 Which of the following statements about damages for breach of contract is correct?

A A claimant who has suffered no actual loss will fail in an action for damages.

B A claimant who has failed to take reasonable steps to mitigate their loss will fail in an action for unliquidated damages.

C A claimant cannot recover unliquidated damages in respect of losses over and above those arising naturally from the breach.

D A claimant is bound by a liquidated damages clause provided it is a genuine attempt to pre-estimate the loss.

139 Which of the following statements about remedies for breach of contract is/are correct?

(i) Where a claim is being made for unliquidated damages, the claimant must take reasonable steps to mitigate their loss.

(ii) Where a claim is being made for liquidated damages, the claimant must take reasonable steps to mitigate their loss.

(iii) Where an action is being brought for the price, the claimant must take reasonable steps to mitigate their loss.

A (i) only

B (ii) only

C (i) and (ii) only

D (i), (ii) and (iii)

140 In breach of contract, S Ltd refused to sell some computer equipment to B Ltd at the agreed price of £10,000. If the type of computer equipment is readily available on the open market at a price of £9,000, which of the following is correct?

A B Ltd is entitled to an order of specific performance, forcing S Ltd to carry out its contract.

B B Ltd is entitled to an order of injunction, preventing S Ltd from selling the equipment to anyone else.

C B Ltd is entitled to nominal damages only.

D B Ltd is not entitled to damages.

141 Systemco Ltd contracted with GHI plc to supply and install a computer system in GHI plc's offices for £50,000. Systemco Ltd performed the contract but the amount due remains outstanding. Systemco Ltd may:

A Recover damages for breach of contract subject to its obligation to take reasonable steps to mitigate its loss

B Apply for an order of specific performance to force GHI plc to pay

C Sue for the price without any obligation to mitigate

D Take back the computer system from GHI plc

142 Which of the following statements in relation to remedies for breach of contract is/are correct?

(i) The remedy of damages will not normally be given where it would cause undue hardship to the defendant.

(ii) A decree of specific performance will not normally be granted where it would cause undue hardship to the defendant.

(iii) A decree of injunction will not normally be granted where it would cause undue hardship to the defendant.

A (i) only

B (ii) only

C (ii) and (iii) only

D (i) and (iii) only

143 Which of the following is incorrect?

A An order for an injunction will not be granted where damages provide an adequate remedy.

B A decree of specific performance will not be granted where damages provide an adequate remedy.

C An order for an injunction will not be granted where the contract is for personal services.

D A decree of specific performance will not be granted where the contract is for personal services.

144 In relation to breach of contract, which of the following is/are correct?

(i) Damages must normally be sought within a reasonable time.

(ii) A decree of specific performance must normally be sought within a reasonable time.

(iii) An injunction must normally be sought within a reasonable time.

A (i) only

B (ii) only

C (ii) and (iii) only

D (i), (ii) and (iii)

145 Which of the following statements relating to remedies for breach of contract is/are incorrect?

(i) If the claimant has acted unfairly they will receive nominal damages only.

(ii) A decree of specific performance will not normally be ordered if the claimant has acted unfairly.

(iii) A decree of injunction will not normally be ordered if the claimant has acted unfairly.

A (i) only

B (ii) only

C (ii) and (iii) only

D (i), (ii) and (iii)

146 Which of the following is/are not available to the innocent party where there has been a breach of a contract to provide personal services?

(i) Damages

(ii) Specific performance

(iii) An action for the price

A (i) only

B (ii) only

C (iii) only

D (ii) and (iii) only

147 Which of the following contracts might be specifically enforceable?

A An accountant has contracted to purchase a number of packets of copier paper for their practice but the seller now refuses to proceed with the contract.

B Scott has contracted to buy a new scooter but he is now refusing to honour the contract.

C Letty has contracted to lease her flat to Ian but has changed her mind and no longer wishes to let it.

D Rowley has contracted to write a book for Publisher, but Rowley is now refusing to write it as he has won the lottery and doesn't now need the money.

SYLLABUS SECTION F: THE LAW OF EMPLOYMENT

148 Which of the following statements suggest that Harriet is an employee in relation to the work she carries out for LMN Ltd?

(i) She carries out work for a number of employers.

(ii) She is required to carry out her work personally and is not free to send a substitute.

(iii) She is entitled to holiday pay and sick pay.

A (i) and (ii) only

B (ii) and (iii) only

C (i) and (iii) only

D (i), (ii) and (iii)

149 Which of the following is/are correct?

(i) An employer is vicariously liable for the torts of employees committed in the course of their employment.

(ii) An employer is vicariously liable for the torts of independent contractors, if they were committed whilst carrying out work for the employer.

(iii) An employer is vicariously liable for the torts of independent contractors, if they were carrying out the instructions of the employer.

A (i) only

B (ii) only

C (iii) only

D (i), (ii) and (iii)

150 Which of the following is/are correct?

(i) A contract of employment must be in writing.

(ii) An employer must provide written particulars of the employment for the employee.

(iii) An employer must provide an itemised pay statement for the employee.

A (i) only

B (ii) only

C (ii) and (iii) only

D (i), (ii) and (iii)

151 An employer must provide an employee with a written statement of particulars of the employment:

A Before the employment commences

B On the first day of the employment

C Within two months of the employment commencing

D Within a reasonable time of the employment commencing

152 Which of the following is/are a source of the terms of a contract of employment?

(i) Custom and practice

(ii) The statutory statement of written particulars

(iii) Common law

A (i) only

B (ii) only

C (i) and (iii) only

D (i), (ii) and (iii)

153 An employee is always entitled to:

A Patent rights on any invention produced by the employee at the workplace

B Use confidential information after the employment has ceased

C Require their employer to give a reference if other work is being sought

D Reasonable and responsible treatment by their employer

154 Which of the following is/are correct?

(i) Full-time employees are entitled to paid leave of at least four weeks a year.

(ii) Full-time employees are entitled to work no more than 48 hours a week, averaged over a 17-week period.

(iii) Full-time employees are entitled to time off for public holidays.

A (i) only

B (ii) only

C (i) and (ii) only

D (i), (ii) and (iii)

155 Which of the following is correct?

A An employer is obliged to provide a careful and honest reference.

B An employer is obliged to provide a safe system of work.

C An employer is obliged to ensure that full-time employees work no more than 48 hours every week of the year.

D An employer is obliged to allow full-time employees at least four weeks paid annual leave plus public holidays.

156 Which of the following is/are normally implied into a contract of employment?

(i) A duty on the employee to exercise reasonable care and skill.

(ii) A duty on the employee to disclose their own wrongdoing.

(iii) A duty on the employee to obey lawful and reasonable orders.

A (i) only

B (ii) only

C (i) and (iii) only

D (i), (ii) and (iii)

157 Which of the following is/are normally implied into a contract of employment?

(i) A duty on the employer to provide work

(ii) A duty on the employer to indemnify the employee for properly incurred expenses

(iii) A duty on the employer to pay wages

A (i) only

B (ii) only

C (ii) and (iii) only

D (i), (ii) and (iii)

158 An employee is always entitled to:

A A reference

B Time off work to attend the wedding of a close relative

C Reasonable remuneration

D Disobey an order from their employer if it is unreasonable

159 In which one of the following situations is an employee not entitled to time off work?

A An employee who has been given notice of their impending redundancy wants to attend an interview for a new job.

B An employee who is training to be the company's safety representative wants to attend a relevant course.

C An employee who intends to leave and has given notice wants to attend an interview for a new job.

D An employee who is a trade union official wants time off to carry out trade union duties.

160 Which one of the following is an employer legally required to do?

A Insure themselves against possible occupational safety liability to employees

B Provide a reference for an employee

C Pay wages to an employee during absence for illness

D Prohibit smoking indoors

161 Gary has been employed by Kay Ltd for eight years. His contract of employment states that if either Kay Ltd or Gary wishes to terminate the contract, each party must give the statutory minimum period of notice.

Which of the following is correct?

A Both Gary and Kay Ltd are entitled to eight weeks' notice.

B Gary is entitled to eight weeks' notice but Kay Ltd is entitled to only one week's notice.

C Both Gary and Kay Ltd are entitled to one month's notice.

D Both Gary and Kay Ltd are entitled to one week's notice.

162 Which of the following statements is/are correct?

(i) Claims by employees for unfair dismissal must normally be presented within six months of termination of employment.

(ii) An employee claiming wrongful dismissal must have at least one year's continuity of employment.

A (i) only

B (ii) only

C Both (i) and (ii)

D Neither

163 An employee suing their employer for unfair dismissal:

A Is bringing a common law claim

B Is claiming damages

C Must normally have been employed by the defendant for at least one year

D Will have their claim rejected if they were given due notice of their dismissal

164 Which of the following is incorrect?

(i) It is automatically unfair to dismiss an employee because they refuse to work in an unsafe workplace.

(ii) It is automatically unfair to dismiss an employee because she becomes pregnant.

(iii) It is automatically unfair to dismiss an employee because of their age.

A (i) only

B (ii) only

C (iii) only

D (ii) and (iii) only

165 Which of the following is incorrect?

A It is automatically unfair to dismiss an employee for trade union activity.

B It is automatically unfair to dismiss an employee who becomes pregnant.

C It is automatically unfair to dismiss an employee who seeks to enforce a statutory right under the Employment Rights Act 1996.

D It is automatically unfair to dismiss an employee without giving the due notice.

166 Which one of the following grounds for dismissal is not automatically unfair?

A The employee complained that the employer was in breach of a statutory health and safety provision.

B The employee was secretly working part-time for a rival company .

C The employee was taking part in the activities of a recognised trade union.

D The employee had become pregnant but could still have done her job until the antenatal care was needed.

167 Which of the following statements is/are correct?

(i) An employee who is offered re-instatement cannot obtain compensation instead.

(ii) An employer must comply with an order of re-engagement if it is practicable to do so.

(iii) Compensation for unfair dismissal can be reduced if the employee's conduct contributed to their dismissal.

A (i) and (ii) only

B (ii) and (iii) only

C (iii) only

D (ii) only

168 Which of the following statements is incorrect?

A An employer is required to keep records of serious accidents.

B An employer is required to set up a safety committee, if requested by the employees' nominated safety representative.

C An employer can defend an action against breach of a health and safety provision if it could not afford to implement that particular measure.

D Health and safety legislation requires employers to take greater care of more vulnerable employees.

169 A Health and Safety Executive inspector has wide powers that may be used against an employer who contravenes health and safety requirements.

Which of the following is/are available to the inspector?

(i) A criminal prosecution

(ii) A civil action for damages

(iii) Specific performance

A (i) only

B (ii) only

C (i) and (iii) only

D (i), (ii) and (iii)

SYLLABUS SECTION G: COMPANY ADMINISTRATION AND FINANCE

170 Which of the following statements about partnerships governed by the Partnership Act 1890 is incorrect?

A In England, a partnership has no existence distinct from the partners.

B A partnership must have a written partnership agreement.

C Partners are jointly and severally liable for the company's debts.

D Each partner is an agent of the company and of the other partners.

171 Which of the following is incorrect?

A A director can also be an employee of the company.

B A shareholder can also be an employee of the company.

C A debenture holder can also be an employee of the company.

D A partner can also be an employee of the company.

172 Which of the following is/are correct?

(i) If a company limited by shares is placed in insolvent liquidation, the company is fully liable for all its debts, but the liability of the shareholders is limited.

(ii) If an unlimited company is placed in insolvent liquidation, the company is fully liable for all its debts, and the liability of the members to contribute to the company's assets is unlimited.

(iii) If a partnership should become insolvent, the partners are jointly and severally liable for the debts of the company.

A (i) only

B (ii) only

C (ii) and (iii) only

D (i), (ii) and (iii)

173 When George started work for Careful Insurance plc as a manager, he contracted with Careful Insurance plc that when his employment with the company ceased he would not solicit or otherwise entice away any of its staff. After George left Careful Insurance plc, he registered a company called George Insurance Ltd. George is its sole director and shareholder. George Insurance Ltd immediately began to solicit members of George's former team.

Which of the following is correct?

A George Insurance Ltd is bound by the contract because it is not a separate entity from George.

B George Insurance Ltd is bound by the contract because contractual obligations of a person who is sole director and shareholder are automatically those of the company.

C George Insurance Ltd is a separate legal entity from George and as such cannot ever be affected by contractual obligations of its members or directors. Therefore George Insurance Ltd cannot be in breach of George's contract with Careful Insurance plc.

D If the court finds that George Insurance Ltd was set up by George to avoid the contract with Careful Insurance plc, it will 'lift the corporate veil' and enforce George's contract with Careful Insurance plc.

174 Which of the following is incorrect?

A A public company limited by shares must offer its shares for public subscription.

B A private company limited by shares cannot invite the public to subscribe for its shares.

C A private company limited by shares cannot invite the public to subscribe for its debentures.

D A public company limited by shares can invite the public to subscribe for its debentures.

175 Phil purchased goods from Thora 'for and on behalf of Phil Ltd'. Phil Ltd was incorporated two days later.

Which of the following is correct?

A The company became liable for the goods immediately it was incorporated.

B Phil is personally liable for the cost of the goods unless the company now ratifies the contract.

C Phil is liable for the cost of the goods but is entitled to be repaid by the company now that it is incorporated.

D Phil is liable for the cost of the goods unless he and Thora agreed otherwise.

176 Which of the following is/are correct?

(i) If a public company trades before it has received a trading certificate from the Registrar of Companies, the contract will be void.

(ii) If a public company borrows money before it has received a trading certificate from the Registrar of Companies, the contract will be void.

(iii) If a public company commences trading without a trading certificate, and fails to meet its obligations, the directors may be held jointly and severally liable for those obligations.

A (i) only

B (ii) only

C (iii) only

D (i), (ii) and (iii)

177 Which of the following is correct?

A The shares of all public limited companies are quoted on the Stock Exchange.

B The company secretary of a private company must be qualified.

C A private limited company can trade immediately it is incorporated.

D A public limited company cannot trade until it has a paid-up share capital of at least £50,000.

178 Which of the following is/are incorrect?

(i) A company's issued share capital must be stated in the capital clause.

(ii) The nominal value of a company's shares must be stated in the capital clause.

(iii) The capital clause may be altered by ordinary resolution.

A (i) only

B (ii) only

C (iii) only

D (i) and (iii) only

179 Which of the following is/are correct?

(i) It is contrary to the Companies Act for a company to be registered with the same name as a company already on the register.

(ii) It is contrary to the Companies Act for a company to be registered with the same registered office as a company already on the register.

(iii) It is contrary to the Companies Act for a company to be registered with the same directors and company secretary as a company already on the register.

A (i) only

B (ii) only

C (iii) only

D (i) and (ii) only

180 What type of business organisation might trade as 'X & Co'?

A A partnership

B A private limited company

C A public limited company

D Any of the above

181 Which of the following is incorrect?

A If a company acts outside its objects clause, the transaction is void.

B Directors who cause a company to act *ultra vires* may be sued by the company for breach of duty.

C The company may ratify an *ultra vires* act by passing a special resolution.

D Any shareholder may apply for an injunction to prevent the directors from taking the company into an *ultra vires* transaction.

182 In relation to companies limited by shares, which of the following is/are correct?

(i) If a company's objects clause states that the company is a 'general commercial company', the company may carry on any lawful trade or business whatsoever.

(ii) A third party who has acted in good faith can enforce an ultra vires transaction against the company.

(iii) Any member can prevent the company from entering into an ultra vires transaction.

A (ii) only

B (iii) only

C (i) and (iii) only

D (i), (ii) and (iii)

183 Which of the following is/are correct?

(i) The Articles of Association form a contract between the company and the board.

(ii) The Articles of Association form a contract between the shareholders and the company and between each shareholder and the other shareholders in respect of all matters contained therein.

(iii) The Articles of Association form a contract between the shareholders and the company and between each shareholder and the other shareholders only in respect of membership matters contained therein.

A (i) only

B (ii) only

C (iii) only

D (i) and (iii) only

184 Which of the following provisions in the Articles of Association of Zed Ltd is/are enforceable by Donna, who is a shareholder and director?

(i) Every share shall carry one vote, except on a resolution to remove a director, in which case that director's shares shall carry three votes each.

(ii) All declared dividends must be paid in cash.

(iii) Every director shall be entitled to be paid £300 for each board meeting attended.

A (i) only

B (ii) only

C (i) and (ii) only

D (i), (ii) and (iii)

185 Which of the following is/are correct?

(i) Procedures for board meetings will be set out in the company's Articles of Association.

(ii) Procedures for board meetings must be set out in the company's Memorandum of Association.

(iii) Usually at board meetings directors have one vote each, a matter is decided upon by simple majority, and the chairperson has a casting vote.

A (i) only

B (ii) only

C (ii) and (iii) only

D (i) and (iii) only

186 Which one of the following cannot be achieved by ordinary resolution?

A An increase of authorised capital in a company's Memorandum of Association

B A reduction of issued share capital

C The dismissal of a director

D A grant of authority to directors to allot shares

187 In relation to private companies, which of the following can alternatively be carried out by the written resolution procedure?

(i) A special resolution to alter the Articles of Association

(ii) An ordinary resolution to remove a director from office

(iii) An elective resolution to dispense with the holding of annual general meetings

A (i) only

B (ii) only

C (i) and (iii) only

D (i), (ii) and (iii)

188 What majority is necessary to pass an ordinary resolution?

A Just 50% of the votes that are cast

B A simple majority of the votes that are cast

C Just 75% of the votes that are cast

D More than 75% of the votes that are cast

189 The board of directors of Wye Ltd is proposing that the articles of association be altered without holding a general meeting of members.

Which of the following is correct?

A The alteration can be achieved provided all the directors sign a copy of a board resolution containing the proposed alteration.

B The alteration can be achieved provided members holding 75% of the voting shares sign a copy of the resolution containing the proposed alteration.

C The alteration can be achieved provided members holding 100% of the voting shares sign a copy of the resolution containing the proposed alteration.

D The Articles of Association can only be altered at a general meeting.

190 An elective resolution can be used to:

A Remove directors from office

B Remove auditors from office

C Remove the statutory requirement to hold an annual general meeting each year

D Remove statutory pre-emption rights where ordinary shares are being issued for cash

191 In relation to companies limited by shares, the statutory minimum period of notice that members must receive of the annual general meeting is:

A 7 days

B 14 days

C 21 days

D 28 days

192 The Companies Act 1985 gives the right to members to requisition an extraordinary general meeting, provided they hold a minimum proportion of the company's issued share capital that carries voting rights. What is that proportion?

A One-twentieth

B One-tenth

C One-quarter

D Three-quarters

193 Before a company limited by shares can hold an extraordinary general meeting at short notice, members holding a certain minimum percentage of the company shares must agree. Which of the following percentages is correct?

A Not less than 5%

B Not less than 10%

C Not less than 75%

D Not less than 95%

194 Which of the following statements regarding the taking and keeping of minutes of board and general meetings is correct?

A It is a statutory requirement for both public and private companies.

B It is a statutory requirement for public companies only.

C It is a statutory requirement for private companies only.

D It is a statutory requirement for neither public nor private companies.

195 Which of the following is incorrect in relation to an increase in a company's authorised share capital?

A The board must resolve to increase the authorised capital.

B The shareholders must pass a resolution to increase the authorised capital.

C Pre-emption rights need not be considered.

D The increase in authorised capital must be confirmed by the court.

196 Which of the following is/are correct?

(i) Directors must be authorised to allot shares by special resolution or by the Articles of Association.

(ii) Directors must be authorised to allot shares by ordinary resolution or by the Articles of Association.

(iii) Directors must be authorised to allot shares by the court.

A (i) only

B (ii) only

C (i) and (iii) only

D (ii) and (iii) only

197 Which of the following is/are correct?

(i) If a public company issues ordinary shares for cash, the shares must first be offered to the existing members.

(ii) If a private company issues ordinary shares for cash, the shares must first be offered to the existing members.

(iii) If a public or private company issues ordinary shares for cash, the shares must first be offered to the directors.

A (i) only

B (ii) only

C (iii) only

D (i) and (ii) only

198 XYZ plc is proposing to issue further ordinary £1 shares. At present, the company's shares have a market value of £3 per share.

Which of the following is/are correct?

(i) XYZ plc can allot the shares at a price of 50p each.

(ii) XYZ plc can allot the shares at a price of £2.50 each.

(iii) XYZ plc can allot the shares at a price of £3.50 each.

A (i) only

B (iii) only

C (ii) and (iii) only

D (i), (ii) and (iii)

199 Which of the following is correct?

A If a private company issues shares for non-cash consideration, the consideration must be independently valued.

B If a public company issues shares for non-cash consideration, the consideration must be independently valued.

C Whenever shares are issued the consideration must be independently valued.

D It is unlawful for shares to be issued for non-cash consideration.

200 Companies limited by shares are subject to the 'maintenance of capital' rule. Which of the following statements regarding the rule is incorrect?

A A company cannot simply return share capital to its shareholders.

B Share capital must be set aside and used to pay creditors in the event of the company becoming insolvent.

C The 'creditor's buffer' represents a pool of funds on which creditors can draw if the company goes into liquidation.

D Share capital may be returned to the shareholders, pursuant to a reduction of capital scheme approved by the court.

201 Which of the following is correct in relation to redeemable shares?

(i) The Articles of Association must include a power to issue redeemable shares.

(ii) They may not be redeemed at a discount to the nominal value.

(iii) They may not be redeemed at a premium to the nominal value.

A (i) only

B (ii) only

C (i) and (ii) only

D (i), (ii) and (iii)

202 BCD Ltd wishes to loan money to Sharon so that she may purchase shares in the company.

Which of the following is correct?

A The proposal is lawful if approved by a special or written resolution and if the correct procedure is followed.

B The proposal is lawful if approved by an ordinary or written resolution and if the correct procedure is followed.

C The proposal is lawful only if the court approves it and if the correct procedure is followed.

D The proposal is unlawful, as a company cannot give financial assistance for the purchase of its own shares.

203 Which of the following does not apply where a private limited company intends to give financial assistance for the acquisition of its own shares?

A The company's Articles must contain a power allowing the company to give financial assistance and the shareholders must pass a resolution to approve the particular financial assistance proposed.

B The board of directors must make a declaration of solvency.

C The financial assistance must be given out of distributable profits if the assistance reduces the company's net assets.

D The financial assistance must be approved by the court.

204 Which of the following does not apply to a private company about to declare a dividend?

A The company's net assets must at least equal the total of its called-up share capital plus undistributable reserves.

B The company must take account of accumulated realised profits.

C The company must take account of accumulated realised losses.

D There must be profits available for dividend.

205 Which of the following statements about company charges is incorrect?

A Charges must be registered at Companies House within 21 days of creation.

B Charges must be registered at the company's registered office.

C Fixed charges take priority over floating charges.

D Later fixed charges take priority over earlier fixed charges.

206 Which of the following is/are correct?

(i) A director is any person occupying the position of director, by whatever name called.

(ii) A shadow director is a person in accordance with whose directions or instructions the directors of a company are accustomed to act.

(iii) A director must hold shares in the company.

A (i) only

B (i) and (ii) only

C (ii) and (iii) only

D (i), (ii) and (iii)

207 Which of the following is/are correct?

(i) The first directors of a company may be appointed by the promoters on incorporation.

(ii) Subsequent directors are appointed in accordance with the company's Memorandum of Association.

(iii) Public companies must appoint a managing director.

A (i) only

B (ii) and (iii) only

C (i) and (iii) only

D (i), (ii) and (iii)

208 Which of the following is/are correct?

(i) The first directors of a company must be named on Form 10, which is submitted to the Registrar on application for registration of the company.

(ii) A person who is an undischarged bankrupt is automatically forbidden by law from being a director of a company.

(iii) A person who has been convicted of fraudulent or wrongful trading is automatically forbidden by law from being a director of a company.

A (i) and (ii) only

B (ii) and (iii) only

C (i) and (iii) only

D (i), (ii) and (iii)

209 The Articles of Association of Exe Ltd provide that Ellen shall be a director of the company for life.

Which of the following is correct?

A Ellen may be removed from office by an ordinary resolution.

B Ellen may be removed from office by an ordinary resolution, but only if the members also pass a special resolution altering the Articles.

C Ellen may be removed from office by an ordinary resolution, but only if she is in breach of duty.

D Ellen may use the provision in the Articles to prevent her removal from office.

210 Which of the following is correct?

A Directors may vote themselves such salary payments as they think fit, irrespective of anything in the company's Articles of Association.

B Directors are not entitled to be paid for their services unless the constitution of the company so provides.

C Directors are entitled to be paid for their services only if such payments are authorised by the members in general meeting.

D Directors must be paid a salary.

211 Directors have a fiduciary duty to act in good faith for the benefit of:

A The members as a whole

B The current members only

C A majority of the members

D Individual members

212 Which of the following is/are correct?

(i) Directors have a fiduciary duty to act in good faith for the benefit of the members as a whole.

(ii) Directors have a fiduciary duty to have regard to the interests of the employees in general as well as to those of the members.

(iii) Directors of an insolvent company have a duty to minimise any potential loss to creditors.

A (i) only

B (ii) only

C (i) and (iii) only

D (i), (ii) and (iii)

213 D is a director of XYZ Ltd and is in breach of his duty of care and skill. As a general rule, action may be taken against him by:

(i) XYZ Ltd

(ii) Individual shareholders of XYZ Ltd

(iii) The board of XYZ Ltd

A (i) only

B (ii) only

C (iii) only

D (i) and (iii) only

214 Wye plc holds its board meetings on the tenth day of each month. At the meeting on 10 April, the board discussed a potential contract with ABC Ltd. On 1 May, Derry, a director of Wye plc, bought shares in ABC Ltd. On 19 May, Wye plc contracted with ABC Ltd. When should Derry have declared his interest to the board of Wye plc?

A 10 April

B 1 May

C 10 May

D 10 June

215 In relation to company law, which of the following is a 'substantial property transaction'?

A The sale of a ship by the company to one of its directors where the value of the transaction exceeds the lesser of £100,000 or 10% of the company's asset value, subject to a minimum value of £2,000.

B The sale of a ship by the company to one of its directors where the value of the transaction exceeds the lesser of £100,000 or 20% of the company's asset value, subject to a minimum value of £2,000.

C The sale of a ship by the company to one of its directors where the value of the transaction exceeds the lesser of £200,000 or 10% of the company's asset value, subject to a minimum value of £2,000.

D The sale of a ship by the company to one of its directors where the value of the transaction exceeds the lesser of £200,000 or 20% of the company's asset value, subject to a minimum value of £2,000.

216 Dan is the sole director of a private limited company. He is also a shareholder. The company is contemplating buying Dan's house for its open market value of £250,000.

Which of the following is/are correct?

(i) The purchase must be approved by the shareholders by ordinary resolution.

(ii) The purchase is unlawful as a sole director is forbidden from contracting with his company.

(iii) Dan is allowed to vote at any general meeting convened to approve the purchase.

A (i) only

B (ii) only

C (iii) only

D (i) and (iii) only

217 Peter is a director of PQR plc. Which of the following is incorrect?

A At common law Peter is required to have expertise in PQR plc's line of business.

B At common law Peter need exercise only the degree of care and skill that would reasonably be expected of a person of his knowledge and experience.

C At common law Peter is not bound to attend all board meetings but he should attend whenever he can.

D At common law Peter is not liable for acts of co-directors unless there are grounds for suspicion or he participates in the wrong.

218 The liquidator of ABC Ltd is contemplating proceedings for wrongful trading under section 214 of the Insolvency Act 1986.

Which of the following is incorrect?

A The liquidator may bring an action against current directors.

B The liquidator may bring an action against former directors.

C If the liquidator is successful, the court may order the defendants to make a contribution to the company's assets.

D If the liquidator is successful, the court may order the defendants to pay a fine.

219 Which of the following provides a defence to proceedings for wrongful trading under section 214 of the Insolvency Act 1986?

A Proof by the defendant that they did not know that there was no reasonable prospect of avoiding insolvent liquidation

B Proof by the defendant that they took every step they ought to have taken with a view to minimising the potential loss to creditors

C Proof by the defendant that they took reasonable steps to minimise the potential loss to creditors

D Proof by the defendant that they had an honest belief that the company's debts would eventually be paid

220 Which of the following statements, in relation to directors of companies limited by shares, is/are incorrect?

(i) The Board is the agent of the shareholders.

(ii) The Board always makes decisions by simple majority of the directors.

(iii) The shareholders cannot interfere with the management of the company unless authorised by the Articles of Association or the law.

A (i) only

B (ii) only

C (iii) only

D (i) and (ii) only

221 XYZ Ltd's articles of association provide that any single borrowing above £1m must be authorised by the members in a general meeting. The Board of XYZ Ltd has caused the company to borrow £3m from BCD Bank. The contract was not put before the general meeting.

Which of the following is normally incorrect?

A The general meeting may ratify the contract.

B The board is liable to the company for breach of duty.

C If BCD Bank was acting in good faith, it may enforce the contract against the board personally.

D If BCD Bank was acting in good faith, it may enforce the contract against the company.

222 While Ian was one of IJK plc's seven directors he defrauded the company of money. This was discovered after Ian ceased to be a director. For good business reasons the board has now decided that IJK plc should not attempt to recover the money from Ian by bringing a civil action against him.

Which of the following is correct?

A The members in a general meeting have statutory power to force the board to change its decision.

B The members in a general meeting have common law power to force the board to change its decision.

C The members have no power to force the board to change its decision unless the Articles of Association so provide.

D The members can sue Ian.

223 Which of the following statements in relation to the company secretary is correct?

A A company secretary of a private or public company is not required to be properly qualified.

B A single member company need not appoint a person to be company secretary.

C A company secretary must be a director of the company.

D A company secretary is an officer of the company.

224 Which of the following statements in relation to the company secretary is incorrect?

A Every company must have a company secretary.

B A company secretary of a public company, but not that of a private company, must be qualified.

C A company secretary may be removed from office by the members in general meeting.

D A company secretary can bind the company in contracts that fall within their actual or apparent authority.

225 Who can petition the court for relief from unfair prejudice under section 459 of the Companies Act 1985?

(i) Any member

(ii) Any director

(iii) The company

A (i) only

B (i) and (ii) only

C (ii) and (iii) only

D (i), (ii) and (iii)

Section 2

ANSWERS TO OBJECTIVE TEST QUESTIONS

SYLLABUS SECTION A: ETHICS AND BUSINESS

1 A

The *Seven Principles of Public Life* apply only to public sector employees in the United Kingdom.

2 D

Accountability involves all of these options.

3 D

Ethics is about how a company does business, not what it does. Its financial viability is not relevant.

4 C

The work of an accountant should meet professional standards. All of the other options are desirable but are not the key attribute.

5 D

Scepticism involves questioning information and seeking supporting evidence before accepting it.

6 B

All of these options give reasons why lifelong learning is important. However, the main reason is the fact that new standards arc regularly issued.

7 A

A code can encourage good behaviour, but it cannot guarantee it, so option D is incorrect. CIMA's Code tells accountants, not stakeholders, what is required of them in terms of behaviour, so option B is incorrect. It focuses on ethical principles rather than legal requirements, so option C is also incorrect.

8 B

A rules-based approach to ethics encourages a tick-box mentality. It is fear driven rather than value driven. It is designed to detect problems rather than prevent them happening in the first place.

9 C

The fundamental principle of objectivity requires accountants to remain free from bias and conflicts of interest.

Option A describes confidentiality. Option B describes professional behaviour. Option D describes professional standards.

10 A

If an accountant is late for a meeting or delivers work late, other members of staff may find that they have to wait around. This is a waste of their employer's resources.

11 B

The mission of IFAC's Ethics Committee was to develop high-quality ethical standards for professional accountants around the world.

12 C

Respect is demonstrated by recognising the rights of others and developing constructive relationships. It is acceptable to disagree with colleagues providing the disagreement does not become personal.

13 C

CIMA's members should ensure that they are professionally competent to take on the work.

14 C

CIMA is a member of IFAC. As such, it cannot apply less stringent standards than those stated in the IFAC Code.

15 C

The two key attributes are independence of mind (being able to reach objective conclusions) and independence in appearance (being seen to be independent).

16 B

An 'independent mind' is one that is free from irrelevant considerations.

17 A

Integrity requires an accountant to be honest. Options C and D describe objectivity. Option B describes confidentiality.

18 B

The ethical principle of due care requires an accountant to perform their work with a high degree of attention and care. Option A describes confidentiality. Option C describes objectivity. Option D describes professional competence.

19 A

The fundamental principles of professional competence and due care requires an accountant to maintain professional knowledge and skill at the level required to ensure clients and employers receive competent professional service.

20 B

Although defining long-term career objectives would help an accountant's career, it would not necessarily have any impact on their ability to act in the public interest.

21 A

The CIMA and IFAC Codes both take a framework-based approach.

22 B

Reliability is not one of the fundamental principles in CIMA's *Code of Ethics*. The five fundamental principles are integrity, objectivity, professional competence and due care, confidentiality and professional behaviour.

23 D

The fundamental principle of professional behaviour requires an accountant to avoid action that could discredit the profession.

24 D

An accountant is required by law to disclose confidential information in the course of legal proceedings or if infringements of the law come to light. This right of disclosure does not require authorisation by the client. An accountant can also disclose information to comply with the quality review of a professional body, if not prohibited by law.

25 C

The five fundamental principles listed in CIMA's *Code of Ethics* are integrity, objectivity, professional competence and due care, confidentiality and professional behaviour.

26 D

Confidentiality is one of the fundamental principles that CIMA's members should comply with, but it is not one of the *Seven Principles of Public Life*.

27 B

A framework-based approach to ethics is values driven rather than fear driven. It is designed to prevent problems happening in the first place rather than to detect them once they have happened. It implies how the individual should behave, rather than giving explicit instructions.

28 A

Omitting information or making false or misleading statements is failing to comply with the fundamental principle of integrity.

29 B

An accountant is required by law to disclose confidential information in the course of legal proceedings or if infringements of the law come to light. This requirement does not depend on the agreement of the client.

30 D

The fundamental principles are integrity, objectivity, professional competence and due care, confidentiality and professional behaviour.

31 C

Honesty is not one of the virtues specified by CIMA.

32 C

Acting diligently in accordance with applicable technical and professional standards is a feature of the fundamental principle of professional competence and due care.

33 C

A framework-based approach to ethics encourages individuals to abide by the spirit of the law rather than simply its letter. It is discretionary rather than mandatory. It is difficult to measure compliance as it does not use a tick-box approach.

34 D

Options (i) and (ii) are describing independence of mind.

SYLLABUS SECTION B: ETHICAL CONFLICT

35 C

Ethical guidelines and standards encourage good practice, but are not required by law. CIMA requires its members to adhere to both its *Code of Ethics* and the IFAC *Code of Ethics*.

36 D

They are all possible consequences.

37 D

All of these outcomes can result from inaccurate or misleading accounts.

38 D

They are all possible consequences.

39 D

Accountants need to demonstrate both independence of mind and independence in appearance. You should therefore declare the potential conflict of interest and ask a colleague to handle the client. To demonstrate propriety, you could also suggest a competitive tender process should be undertaken.

40 B

A relationship with a colleague is not, in itself, a cause for concern. However, you should inform your manager about the relationship. It may also be advisable to suggest that the password control system is changed. Even if the relationship does not last, your manager will be able to continue to trust your judgment because of your openness about the situation. Keeping the relationship a secret is not advisable (and probably not realistically possible), it might lead to one or other of you being dismissed under suspicion of potential collusion or fraud.

41 A

You should query your manager's suggestion, as the timing of the entertainment might be interpreted as an inducement to the auditors. You could suggest it would be easier and more appropriate to do this after the audit has been completed.

42 B

You need to speak to your manager about your concerns and request support or training to gain the necessary skills and experience to undertake your new role.

43 D

Delia should challenge the request. She should not book the sales until the business has received an actual order. To do otherwise would mean that the year end accounts would be incorrect.

44 A

The long association of a senior member of the assurance team with the assurance client is an example of a familiarity threat. The other three are all examples of self-review threats as they involve situations where a previous judgment needs to be re-evaluated.

45 A

A threat that may occur as a result of the financial or other interests of a professional accountant or of an immediate or close family member is known as a self-interest threat. A familiarity threat occurs where, because of a close relationship, an accountant becomes too sympathetic to the interests of others.

46 B

Leadership that stresses the importance of compliance with the fundamental principles is an example of a company-wide safeguard in the work environment.

47 D

The threat that may occur when, because of a close relationship, an accountant becomes too sympathetic to the interests of others is a familiarity threat.

48 C

Being threatened with litigation is an example of an intimidation threat.

49 B

Having a close business relationship with a client is an example of a self-interest threat.

50 D

The holding of a client's money creates threats to compliance with the fundamental principles. An accountant who is entrusted with money belonging to a client should ensure that it is kept separate from personal and company assets.

51 A

Long association with business contacts influencing business decisions is an example of a familiarity threat.

52 A

An accountant in a position to influence financial reporting having a close family member who is in a position to benefit from that influence is an example of a familiarity threat.

53 D

Being able to manipulate information in order to gain financially is an example of a self-interest threat.

54 B

The most ethical decision is not always the most popular one.

55 C

Ignoring the issue will not help you to resolve it.

56 D

The least likely scenario is for your colleague's manager to applaud his bullying behaviour.

57 C

Disclosing to those charged with governance of the client the nature of services provided and extent of fees charged is an example of an engagement-specific safeguard.

SYLLABUS SECTION C: CORPORATE GOVERNANCE

58 C

The imposition of a three-year maximum term on service contracts relates to executive directors, not non-executive directors.

59 A

The Sarbanes-Oxley Act applies to all publicly traded companies listed in the United States. It does not distinguish between United States companies and foreign companies.

60 C

The original Combined Code on Corporate Governance incorporated the recommendations of the Cadbury, Greenbury and Hampel reports. The Turnbull Report was published at a later date.

61 A

FTSE 350 listed companies require half their board to be independent non-executive directors.

62 D

According to the Combined Code, none of these individuals could be regarded as independent.

63 D

The term stakeholder is very wide. It encompasses everyone who may be affected, directly or indirectly, by a company's actions.

64 A

The Combined Code is not legislation. It is therefore not mandatory. Companies are required to either comply with the Combined Code or explain why they have not done so. Therefore a company that explains why it has not complied with the Combined Code's recommendations would nonetheless be complying with it.

65 D

Directors owe a duty of care and skill to the shareholders as a body. The duty is enforceable by the company. Directors do not owe a duty of care to the public at large or to creditors, although both of these categories are encompassed by the term 'stakeholder' and should therefore be considered when deciding how to act.

66 A

In the United Kingdom, directors are mainly concerned with the interests of the shareholders. They must take account of the interests of employees and creditors, but neither of these categories is routinely represented on the board.

67 C

The Combined Code gives rise to neither civil nor criminal liability, so option D is incorrect. Wrongful trading occurs where directors cause the company to continue trading where insolvency appears inevitable, so option A is incorrect. The Combined Code is not mandatory, so directors cannot be disqualified for failing to observe it.

68 C

In the United Kingdom, companies generally utilise the unitary board system. The examples given, that is an all-executive board, a majority executive board and a majority non-executive board, are all types of unitary boards.

69 D

The Combined Code recommends the use of board committees made up of non-executive directors. Audit, remuneration and nominations committees are recommended, but not planning committees.

70 B

The Greenbury Committee recommended that annual bonuses should not be pensionable.

71 D

A company's internal regulations are found in the articles of association. These usually provide for board decisions to be decided by a simple majority of the votes.

72 B

The Greenbury Committee was primarily concerned with directors' remuneration.

73 C

Directors' duties are owed to the company as a whole.

74 D

The Hampel Committee recommended that the remuneration of executive directors should be based upon the recommendations of a remuneration committee comprised entirely of non-executive directors.

75 D

The rules of corporate governance are best practice. They are not legally enforceable.

76 A

The Combined Code applies to all listed companies.

77 D

A two-tier board structure comprises a management board and a supervisory board.

78 D

The chairman is responsible for leadership of the board and setting its agenda.

79 D

The common law duty of care is now equivalent to the statutory test applied in cases of wrongful trading – option (i). Options (ii) and (iii) derive from the case of *Re City Equitable Fire Insurance Co Ltd.*

80 D

The Smith Report dealt with the role and responsibilities of audit committees.

SYLLABUS SECTION D: COMPARISON OF ENGLISH LAW WITH ALTERNATIVE LEGAL SYSTEMS

81 B

An appeal from the County Court will normally go to the Court of Appeal.

82 B

The principal objective of the criminal law is to regulate behaviour by the threat of punishment. Victims may be able to obtain compensation through the civil courts.

83 B

This option contains two civil law words, i.e. action and damages. The other options all contain words that describe criminal proceedings, e.g. prosecution, accused and offence.

84 B

The highest court in England is the House of Lords.

85 B

Equity prevails over the common law. Acts of Parliament can overrule both common law and equity. Equitable remedies are discretionary.

86 D

Parliament can delegate law-making powers to **any** person it sees fit.

87 B

Where there is a conflict, *ratio decidendi* is always superior to *obiter dicta.*

The *ratio decidendi* of a higher court overrides that of a lower court.

88 B

European Union law overrides all forms of English law.

89 C

Unlike the United Kingdom Parliament, the European Parliament has no law-making powers – so (iii) is wrong. European Union directives are a blueprint for new laws, which must then be made into measures of law by each and every member state – so (i) is wrong.

90 A

European Union regulations become law in the member states without need for further action. Directives must be enacted by the member states before they come into effect. Decisions and resolutions are not binding.

91 C

The three essential elements of the tort of negligence are duty of care (option A), breach of duty (option B) and resultant loss (option D).

92 A

The three essential elements of the tort of negligence are duty of care (option A), breach of duty (option B) and resultant loss. Intention to cause loss/harm/injury/damage is not an essential element.

93 C

To be recoverable, losses must be reasonably foreseeable.

94 B

As a general rule, auditors owe a duty of care only to the company that they are auditing, not to investors and others who might rely on the audit report – *Caparo Inds v Dickman*. But see the distinguishing case of *ADT v Binder Hamlyn*.

Note that Company plc could also sue Anne for breach of contract.

95 C

Option A describes the defence of *volenti non fit injuria* (often called 'consent'). It is a complete defence in that, if it succeeds, the defendant escapes liability altogether. Contributory negligence, in contrast, is a partial defence in that the claimant's damages are reduced. (A classic example of the application of contributory negligence is failure to wear a seat-belt in car accidents.)

96 C

The other three options correctly describe the plea of *res ipsa loquitur*.

97 A

In the tort of negligence, damages are payable in respect of reasonably foreseeable losses. Answer D in this question is a reference to the decision in *Hadley v Baxendale* on the amount of damages in a case of breach of contract.

98 C

The facts of the *Caparo* case were distinguished from those of the earlier cases. The term 'reversing' is used when a case is overturned on appeal. So option A is wrong. The term 'overruling' is used in similar situations to 'reversing'. So option D is wrong. The term 'disapproving' is used to express an opinion on an earlier decision. So option B is also wrong.

99 A

The *ratio decidendi* is the reason for the decision. It has nothing to do with the facts of the case. So option C is incorrect.

100 D

The Five Pillars of Islam are obligatory, meritorious, permissible, reprehensible and forbidden.

101 C

The European Union currently consists of 25 member states.

102 C

The European Court of Justice deals with disputes involving European Union laws. The International Court of Justice deals with disputes between nations. The United Nations does not prosecute individuals.

SYLLABUS SECTION E: THE LAW OF CONTRACT

103 A

A contract of guarantee must be evidenced in writing. Companies can make oral contracts as well as written ones. An employment contract can also be oral, however, a written statement must be provided to the employee within two months of the commencement of employment.

104 B

A contract for the sale of land must be in writing. However, the partnership agreement and employment contract can be made orally.

105 D

Commercial transactions are presumed to be legally binding. Legal relations are not presumed in family, domestic and social arrangements. These presumptions are not rebutted simply because the agreement is in writing.

106 A

The advertisement is an invitation to treat. B plc has made an offer, which Office Supplies Ltd can refuse to accept.

107 C

B has requested further information. Therefore they have neither accepted nor rejected the offer at this stage.

108 B

The postal rule does not apply to acceptance by fax. Therefore the general rule, that acceptance is effective when it reaches the offeree, applies.

109 C

The postal rule only applies to the acceptance of an offer. A counter-offer means that the original offer can no longer be accepted. Acceptance must be communicated for it to be effective.

110 C

The promise to perform an existing duty cannot amount to consideration. Past consideration is also insufficient. A peppercorn can amount to consideration as it has some value. It is not necessary for the consideration to be adequate (i.e. of equal value).

111 A

Y gave consideration on Saturday when he made his promise of payment. If he fails to pay at the end of the month he commits a breach of contract.

112 C

Option (ii) – a claimant can apply for rescission in all actions for mis-representation. However, as an equitable remedy, it will not be granted in all circumstances.

113 C

Rescission is an equitable remedy which may be refused by the court.

114 C

Rescission is an equitable remedy. It may be denied by the court if the claimant has acted unfairly.

115 D

Option A is wrong because rescission has the effect of restoring the parties to their original pre-contractual positions.

Option B is wrong because rescission is an equitable remedy, and thus, like all equitable remedies, it is given at the discretion of the court: there is no entitlement.

Option C is wrong. There is no entitlement to damages where the misrepresentation is innocent, although the court has a discretion to award damages in lieu of rescission under s2(2) Misrepresentation Act 1967.

Option D is an application of the maxim of equity 'He who comes to Equity must come with clean hands'.

116 B

The court cannot imply terms in order to make the contract fairer. However, terms may be implied into the contract by statute, previous business dealings or business efficacy.

117 B

If a condition is breached, the innocent party can choose to terminate the contract and claim damages. If a warranty is breached, the innocent party can only claim damages.

118 B

If STU Ltd takes option (iii) – called affirmation of the contract – it may nevertheless claim damages.

119 B

If a condition is breached, the innocent party can choose to terminate the contract and claim damages. However, a contract cannot be terminated if it has been affirmed.

120 A

Where goods are sold in the course of a business, s14(2) Sale of Goods Act 1979 implies a condition into the contract that the goods are of satisfactory quality. Knowledge, negligence or fault of the seller is immaterial.

121 D

To be valid, an exemption clause must be agreed by the parties. If it is included in a signed contract, it is generally treated as having been agreed. However, the clause is not binding if the signature was induced by fraud or misrepresentation.

122 A

The Unfair Contract Terms Act 1977 declares such exclusions to be void.

123 A

The Unfair Contract Terms Act 1977 states that clauses exempting liability for breach of the Sale of Goods Act's s13, s14 and s15 implied terms are void unless reasonable in a non-consumer transaction such as this. The Unfair Contract Terms Act also states that it is for the party seeking to rely on the clause to prove that it is reasonable.

124 C

A person in business cannot exclude or restrict liability for death or personal injury resulting from negligence. There are no exceptions to this rule.

125 A

The Unfair Terms in Consumer Contracts Regulations 1999 apply only to standard form contracts for the supply of goods and services.

126 B

The basic principle of contract law is that if you choose to agree by contract to do something then you must do it: if you do it then you get your money; if you don't do it then you're in breach of contract – straightforward and simple! So option B is the application of this basic principle to these facts.

The doctrine of frustration is an exception to the basic principle in that if it comes into play it lawfully excuses non-performance. Clearly the doctrine is not applicable here since it's Decor's fault that the Health and Safety Executive made the prohibition order. So option D is not correct.

127 A

If you are unsure of this, look again at the topic 'discharge by performance'. Note that 'substantial performance' implies 'performance of all obligations but with defects'.

128 A

To be frustrated, a contract must have become impossible to perform after it was made.

129 B

As to option (iii), although in general 'illegality' frustrates a contract, this is not the case here because, amongst other things, it is the hotel owner's fault that there has been a breach of safety regulations.

130 D

A fine is not a remedy for breach of contract.

131 C

Damages is a common law remedy. Specific performance and injunction are equitable remedies.

132 C

Option (iii) correctly describes the compensatory purpose of damages.

133 C

Regarding option (iii), very exceptionally damages are awarded for loss of enjoyment and distress. This is the case for contracts for the provision of a holiday trip, etc, where the contract is, in essence, selling enjoyment.

134 D

Damages are not intended to punish the party in breach of contract.

135 D

Nominal damages may be awarded if the claimant has suffered no actual loss.

136 D

The court will award an amount that is a genuine pre-estimate of the loss, even if the actual loss is greater or smaller.

137 D

Under the second limb of the rule in *Hadley v Baxendale*, a claim for abnormal losses is permitted if those losses were within the reasonable contemplation of the parties at the time the contract was made.

138 D

A claimant who has suffered no actual loss will be awarded nominal damages – option A is incorrect.

If a claimant fails to take reasonable steps to mitigate (i.e. minimise) their loss, the court will assess their damages on the basis of what would have been their loss had they actually taken such steps – so option B is incorrect.

Option C is incorrect because the second limb of the rule in *Hadley v Baxendale*, dealing with remoteness of loss, allows recovery of abnormal losses if they were within the reasonable contemplation of the parties at the time when the contract was made.

139 A

Liquidated damages will always be paid if they are a genuine pre-estimate of the loss.

In an action for the price, a claimant who has performed their obligations under a contract is simply suing the other party for the price due to be paid under the terms of the contract.

140 C

This question is testing your understanding of the principle that damages are available as of right; and that, where there is no actual loss, damages must therefore be nominal.

As to options A and B, they are wrong for at least two reasons. First, since they are equitable remedies there is no entitlement to them. Second, damages are, in the circumstances, obviously an adequate remedy.

141 C

The breach of contract disclosed by the facts is failure to pay the price. In such a circumstance the only remedy of the innocent party is 'action for the price'. Mitigation of damages is irrelevant.

142 C

Specific performance and injunction are equitable remedies that are awarded at the discretion of the court. They are therefore only awarded where it is just and equitable to do so. Damages is a common law remedy that is available as of right.

143 C

The case of *Warner Brothers Pictures Inc v Nelson* is evidence that the court will not grant an injunction where the contract is for personal services.

144 C

The only restriction on damages is the Limitation Act 1980 (six years for most contracts).

145 A

Specific performance and injunction are equitable remedies that are awarded at the discretion of the court. They are therefore only awarded where it is just and equitable to do so. Damages is a common law remedy that is available as of right.

146 B

Where the contract is one for personal services, all the remedies for breach of contract are potentially available with the exception of specific performance.

147 C

Specific performance is commonly given of contracts for the sale or lease of land because, since land is unique, damages are an inadequate remedy. Specific performance is not given of contracts for the sale of goods (except in the exceptional case of unique goods) because damages are an adequate remedy. This is why both options A and B are incorrect. Option D is incorrect because specific performance is never given of a contract for personal services.

SYLLABUS SECTION F: THE LAW OF EMPLOYMENT

148 B

An employee is usually required to carry out the work personally. Employees are also entitled to holiday pay and sick pay. An independent contractor will usually work for a number of clients.

149 A

Employers are not vicariously liable for torts committed by independent contractors.

150 C

Options (ii) and (iii) are requirements of the Employment Rights Act 1996.

151 C

This is a statutory requirement of the Employment Rights Act 1996.

152 D

Although the statutory statement of written particulars is not the contract of employment, it provides evidence as to what the employer believes to be the terms of the contract: thus it is a source of the terms.

Other sources include statute and collective bargaining agreements.

153 D

Option A – inventions produced as part of the employee's work belong to the employer not the employee. Option B – a restrictive covenant may prevent an employee using confidential information. Option C – there is no legal obligation on the employer to provide a reference.

154 C

The Working Time Regulations 1998 give entitlement to a 48-hour maximum working week and four weeks paid holiday for full-time employees.

155 B

Option A is wrong because there is no general obligation to provide a reference – although it is true that any reference provided must be honest and given with reasonable carc.

Option C is wrong is wrong because the statutory maximum 48-hour working week is averaged over a 17-week period.

Any time off for public holidays allowed by an employer is not in addition to the statutory minimum four weeks annual leave – option D is wrong.

156 C

An employee is under a duty to exercise reasonable care and skill and to obey lawful and reasonable orders.

157 C

At common law there is no general duty to provide work.

158 D

There is nothing in statute nor at common law that gives employees in general a right to a reference – thus option A is wrong.

Option B is wrong – there is nothing in statute nor the common law giving a right to time off for such things as weddings, study leave, FA cup finals, etc.

There is a common law duty of an employer to pay reasonable remuneration but this becomes relevant only if the parties have not expressly agreed the amount of pay – so option C is wrong.

159 C

Trade union officials and health and safety representatives are entitled to time off work to carry out their duties. An employee who is being made redundant is entitled to time off work under the Employment Rights Act 1996 to look for a new job. However, this right does not extend to employees who have chosen to leave their employment.

160 A

An employer is required to insure against occupational safety liability. They may agree to options B, C and D, but they are not required to do so.

161 B

The statutory minimum period of notice that an employer must give depends on the length of employment, namely:

- 1 week where the employment has lasted 1 month but less than 2 years
- 1 week for each complete year where the employment has lasted 2 years but less than 12 years
- 12 weeks where employment has lasted 12 years.

The statutory minimum period of notice that an employee must give is 1 week, irrespective of the period of employment.

162 D

Actions for unfair dismissal must be started within three months of the termination of employment. There is no minimum length of employment for a claim of wrongful dismissal.

163 C

The other three options are appropriate to wrongful dismissal, not unfair dismissal.
The one-year qualifying period for unfair dismissal does not apply where the employee was dismissed for an inadmissible reason.

164 C

It is automatically unfair to dismiss an employee due to pregnancy, childbirth or health and safety matters.

165 D

If you were not sure about this, go back to your source material and look up the 'automatically unfair' reasons (also called 'inadmissible' reasons because they are reasons that the Employment Rights Act 1996 says can *never* be used by an employer to justify a dismissal as fair).

166 B

Working part-time for a rival company could potentially be justified as a reason for dismissal, provided that the manner of the dismissal is fair.

167 C

A tribunal will only order re-instatement or re-engagement where the employee wants it. An employer cannot be forced to comply with an order for re-engagement. However, if they do not do so, further compensation will be awarded.

168 C

Health and safety legislation requires employers to ensure 'so far as is reasonably practicable' the health and safety of their employees. However, the cost of implementing a particular measure is only relevant if it is disproportionately high in relation to the risk of injury.

169 A

The three possible statutory powers of the Health and Safety Executive are:

- to launch a criminal prosecution (resulting, for example, in a fine or possibly imprisonment)
- to issue an improvement notice
- to issue a prohibition notice.

SYLLABUS SECTION G: COMPANY ADMINISTRATION AND FINANCE

170 B

A partnership does not require a written agreement. However, in order to avoid future disputes, it is usually advisable for the agreement to be in writing.

171 D

A partnership has no legal existence distinct from the partners and it is not possible to be an employee of yourself.

172 D

Companies are fully liable for their debts. However, the liability of the shareholders depends on whether the company is limited or unlimited. The liability of the shareholders of a limited company is limited to the amount of capital they have agreed to contribute. The shareholders of an unlimited company have unlimited liability. The partners of a partnership are fully liable for the debts of the partnership.

173 D

This question is based on *Gilford Motor Co v Horne* where the court, exceptionally, lifted the veil of incorporation.

174 A

A private company must raise capital (whether share or loan) privately. It is only the public company that is allowed to tap the resources of the investing public – but this does not mean that it must do so.

175 D

A company cannot enter into or ratify a contract entered into before the date of its incorporation.

176 C

Contracts entered into **after** the issue of the certificate of incorporation but **before** the issue of the trading certificate are **not void**.

177 C

Public limited companies are not necessarily quoted on the Stock Exchange. The company secretary of a public company must be qualified. The issued share capital of a public company must be at least £50,000, but it does not necessarily have to be fully-paid up.

178 A

It is the authorised capital that must be stated in the capital clause, not the issued capital.

179 A

A company cannot be registered with the same name as a company already on the register.

180 D

Be careful to differentiate **business** (or **trading**) name from **registered** name.

181 A

Section 35 of the Companies Act 1985 provides that an *ultra vires* transaction is not void for being *ultra vires*.

182 D

An *ultra vires* transaction can be enforced by a third party. A member can obtain an injunction to prevent the directors from entering into an *ultra vires* transaction. The objects clause may be drafted widely to enable a company to carry on any lawful business.

183 C

The Articles of Association form a contract between the members and the company and the members amongst themselves in their capacity as members.

184 C

Donna can only enforce Articles affecting her rights as a member.

185 D

A company's internal regulations are found in the Articles of Association. These usually provide for board decisions to be decided by a simple majority of the votes.

186 B

A reduction of issued share capital requires a special resolution.

187 C

The written resolution procedure can be used for any resolution except the removal of the auditor and the removal of a director.

188 B

Simply, more than 50% of the votes that are cast.

189 C

A written resolution always requires all voting members to sign in favour.

190 C

An elective resolution can be used to dispense with the statutory requirement to hold an annual general meeting each year.

191 C

The annual general meeting requires 21 days' written notice.

192 B

An extraordinary general meeting can be requisitioned by members holding at least one-tenth of the issued and paid up shares carrying voting rights.

193 D

The percentage for an extraordinary general meeting is 100%.

194 A

All companies must take and retain minutes of board and general meetings.

195 D

Pre-emption rights are relevant to an increase in issued (not authorised) share capital.

196 B

An ordinary resolution is needed to authorise the directors to allot shares.

197 D

All companies, whether public or private, must first offer shares to the existing members if the shares are being issued for cash.

198 C

Shares may not be issued at a discount to the **nominal** value, thus option (i) would be illegal.

199 B

Non-cash consideration must be independently valued in the case of shares being issued by a public company.

200 B

The money raised by an issue of shares is not set aside for the creditors.

201 A

Shares must not be **issued** at a discount, but may be **redeemed** at any value.

202 A

As a general rule, it is illegal for a company to give financial assistance (e.g. a loan) for the acquisition of its own shares. But there are exceptions where it can be lawful. The exception that is relevant here is where a private company can give financial assistance for any reason provided the correct procedure is followed. Amongst other things, a special resolution is required.

203 D

The resolution must be a special resolution (or a written one). The financial assistance does not need court approval.

204 A

The net assets test – given at option A – applies to public companies, not to private companies.

205 D

Similar charges rank in order of creation.

206 B

Many directors hold shares in the company for which they work, but there is no legal requirement to do so.

207 A

Subsequent directors are appointed in accordance with the Articles of Association.

208 A

Fraudulent or wrongful trading may potentially disqualify a director.

209 A

Under section 303 of the Companies Act 1985, a company may by ordinary resolution remove a director before the expiration of their period of office notwithstanding anything in its Articles of Association.

210 B

Directors' remuneration must be authorised in accordance with the Articles of Association.

211 A

The directors owe their duty to the members as a whole.

212 D

Directors who fail to have regard to (iii) may find that they are liable for wrongful trading.

213 A

Directors' duties are owed to the company as a whole.

214 C

Derry should have declared his interest in ABC Ltd at the first board meeting after he became aware of his interest in the proposed contract.

215 A

A substantial property transaction is a sale of a non-cash asset between a company and a director where the value exceeds the lesser of £100,000 or 10% of the company's assets, subject to a minimum value of £2,000.

216 D

This is a substantial property transaction. It must be approved by the shareholders in a general meeting. As a shareholder, Dan is allowed to vote.

217 A

Options B, C and D are correct statements of the common law duty of care and skill.

218 D

Wrongful trading is not a criminal offence – contrast with fraudulent trading.

219 B

Option B reflects the wording of the Insolvency Act 1986.

220 C

Option (i) is incorrect because the board is the agent of the company, not of the shareholders.

Regarding option (ii) – proceedings at board meetings are regulated by the company's Articles of Association: the articles may provide for simple majority decisions, but not necessarily.

221 C

Section 35A of the Companies Act 1985 allows a third party to enforce such a contract against the company.

222 C

This is a difficult question. Normally it is only the company that may bring an action against the defaulting director.

223 D

A company secretary of a public company must be qualified, but there is no such requirement for a private company. A single member company must have a company secretary, who cannot be the sole member. The company secretary may or may not be a director.

224 C

A company secretary is usually appointed and removed by the directors.

225 A

Any member may complain of unfair prejudice.

5 How does the framework-based approach to ethics differ from the rules-based approach?

A The framework-based approach uses legal language.

B The framework-based approach requires a detailed rule book.

C The framework-based approach sets out rules covering all eventualities.

D The framework-based approach sets out general guidelines.

6 What is the name of the United Kingdom's independent regulator for corporate reporting and governance?

A Accounting Standards Board

B Financial Reporting Council

C Auditing Practices Board

D Professional Oversight Board for Accountancy

7 Which of the following is not one of the *Seven Principles of Public Life* issued by the Committee on Standards in Public Life?

A Courtesy

B Openness

C Integrity

D Leadership

8 'A professional accountant should comply with relevant laws and regulations and should avoid any action that discredits the profession.' Which of the fundamental principles does this sentence relate to?

A Professional competence and due care

B Integrity

C Professional behaviour

D Objectivity

9 The concept of being able to be trusted by others and being able to deliver what has been agreed when it has been agreed is a description of which of the following virtues?

A Timeliness

B Responsibility

C Courtesy

D Reliability

10 Which of the following is not one of the personal qualities and virtues specifically sought by CIMA?

A Courtesy

B Timeliness

C Respect

D Selflessness

11 A code of ethics is likely to achieve which of the following?

(i) Eliminate the need for legislation on ethical issues

(ii) Encourage employees to take a consistent approach to ethical issues

(iii) Tell the employees what kind of behaviour is expected of them

A (i), (ii) and (iii)

B (i) and (ii) only

C (ii) and (iii) only

D (i) and (iii) only

12 Linda produces a quarterly profit and loss account for her managing director. The sales director is responsible for supplying the turnover figure. However, the information he provides consists simply of a list of invoices and does not come from any accounting system.

Does Linda have an ethical dilemma?

A No, responsibility for the accuracy of the turnover figure lies with the sales director.

B No, Linda is exhibiting professional behaviour.

C Yes, Linda cannot rely on the sales director to supply accurate information.

D Yes, the list used by Linda creates an integrity issue.

13 Your employer is having liquidity problems and has reached its overdraft limit. The finance director has asked you to review the company's accounting policies to see if a change could improve the presentation of the financial accounts, which are supplied on a monthly basis to the bank. From an ethical perspective, what is the most appropriate action for you to take?

A Seek advice from your professional body.

B Do as requested and seek advice afterwards.

C Do as requested.

D Go off sick.

14 Promoting shares in a listed entity when that entity is a financial statement audit client is an example of which kind of threat?

A A self-interest threat

B A self-review threat

C An advocacy threat

D A familiarity threat

15 Which of the following statements is/are true?

(i) Governance refers to the way in which an organisation is run.

(ii) Social responsibility refers to how an organisation manages its relationships with its shareholders.

A (i) only

B (ii) only

C Both

D Neither

16 Which of the following is not an example of a company-wide safeguard in the work environment?

A Rotating senior assurance team personnel

B Policies to monitor the reliance on revenue received from a single client

C Advising staff of those clients and related entities from which they must be independent

D A disciplinary mechanism to promote compliance with policies and procedures

17 The country in which you are working temporarily has a piece of legislation that is in conflict with the IFAC *Code of Ethics*. What should you do?

A Obey the *Code of Ethics* because it is a requirement of your profession.

B Obey the law because it is mandatory.

C Discuss the matter with your boss and abide by their decision.

D Avoid dealing with the issue as you are only in the country temporarily.

18 Which one of the following correctly describes the relationship between ethics, governance, law and social responsibility in an organisation?

A Legislation is designed to be compatible with an organisation's code of ethics.

B Ethics and governance are mutually exclusive.

C Ethical behaviour is mandatory, whereas social responsibility is discretionary.

D Social responsibility policies should be consistent with a company's values and code of ethics.

19 Which of the following does the Combined Code apply to?

A All listed companies

B Small listed companies only

C Large listed companies only

D All companies

20 What does a two-tier board comprise?

A An executive board and a management board

B A non-executive board and a management board

C A supervisory board and an employee representation board

D A management board and a supervisory board

21 Which of the following is not a recommendation of the Combined Code?

A The chairmen of the audit, remuneration and appointments committees should attend the annual general meeting.

B A board audit committee should be established.

C The roles of chairman and chief executive should be combined.

D At least half of the board should be made up of independent non-executive directors.

22 Which of the following was not a recommendation of the Cadbury Committee?

A Executive directors' service contracts should not provide for notice periods in excess of one year.

B An audit committee consisting of a majority of non-executive directors should be established.

C The same person should not act as both chief executive and chairman.

D The appointment of all executive directors should be vetted by a nomination committee made up of the company's non-executive directors.

23 Which of the following statements is incorrect?

A A unitary board structure means there is one board responsible for both management and governance.

B The main criticism of an all-executive board is that the directors appear to be monitoring and supervising their own performance.

C Board structures in the United States are generally two-tier in structure.

D In Germany employees are represented at board level.

24 Which of the following statements is not a reason in favour of having a strong corporate governance regime?

A Good governance prevents companies from being dominated by a chief executive.

B Good governance reduces the risk of misleading financial reporting.

C Good governance adds to confidence in the stock market.

D Good governance eliminates the need for legislation.

25 Which of the following statements in respect of the Sarbanes-Oxley Act are correct?

(i) The Act requires the chief executive officer and chief finance officer to certify the accuracy of their company's financial statements.

(ii) The Act established the Public Company Accounting Oversight Board to oversee the auditing of public companies.

(iii) The Act prohibits a company from terminating the employment of any individual reporting a securities fraud.

A (i) and (ii)

B (i) and (iii)

C (ii) and (iii)

D (i), (ii), and (iii)

26 Which of the following does not have civil jurisdiction?

A The County Court

B The Crown Court

C The Court of Appeal

D The House of Lords

27 Which of the following is/are correct?

(i) In the event of a conflict between equity and the common law, equity prevails.

(ii) An Act of Parliament can overrule any common law or equitable rule.

(iii) European Union regulations can override equity.

A (i) and (ii) only

B (ii) and (iii) only

C (i) and (iii) only

D (i), (ii) and (iii)

28 Which of the following is the superior source of law?

A *Ratio decidendi* of the House of Lords

B *Obiter dicta* of the House of Lords

C A statutory instrument

D A European Union regulation

29 Which one of the following European Union bodies is responsible for proposing new legislation that is to apply to its member states?

A The European Parliament

B The Court of Justice of the European Communities

C The European Commission

D The Council of the European Union

30 Which of the following must a Bill receive in order to become an Act of Parliament?

A The Assent of the Prime Minister

B The Assent of the Government

C Royal Assent

D The Assent of the High Court

31 Which of the following is not an essential element of the tort of negligence?

A The existence of a duty of care

B Breach of the duty of care

C A contractual relationship between the parties

D Loss caused by the breach

32 If, in the tort of negligence, the defendant is able to establish that the claimant was partly responsible for their own injuries:

A The claimant cannot recover any compensation from the defendant

B The court will reduce the damages payable to the claimant

C The court will award nominal damages only

D The court will dismiss the case

33 Which of the following countries does not have a system of codified civil law?

A France

B Germany

C Poland

D Denmark

34 S Ltd displays a video telephone in its shop window priced at £199. Burt goes into the shop and says he will buy the video telephone for £199. S Ltd says it has been wrongly priced and refuses to sell it.

Which of the following is correct?

A A contract has been made between S Ltd and Burt.

B No contract has been made because Burt makes an offer to S Ltd which S Ltd has rejected.

C No contract has been made because Burt makes a counter-offer which S Ltd has rejected.

D No contract has been made because there is no offer.

35 Which of the following is/are incorrect?

(i) A person must know of an offer before they can accept it.

(ii) The postal rule always applies to the revocation of an offer by posted letter.

(iii) The postal rule always applies to the acceptance of an offer by posted letter.

A (i) only

B (ii) only

C (ii) and (iii) only

D (i), (ii) and (iii)

36 D owes £5,000 to C.

Which of the following is correct?

A If C agrees to accept less than the full amount due from D, the debt is discharged at common law.

B If C agrees to accept less than the full amount due from D, they may go back on their word and recover the balance from D at common law.

C If C agrees to accept less than the full amount due from T, a third party, thcy may go back on their word and recover the balance from D at common law.

D If C had freely agreed to accept less than the full amount due from D before it was due for payment, they may go back on their word and recover the balance once the due date for payment arrives.

37 In relation to misrepresentation, which of the following statements is correct?

A As a general rule, failure to disclose relevant facts amounts to misrepresentation.

B The misrepresentee cannot claim damages if they have affirmed the contract.

C A person cannot sue for misrepresentation if it did not induce them to contract.

D A half-truth cannot amount to a misrepresentation.

38 A Ltd has been induced to enter into a contract with B Ltd by the latter's fraudulent misrepresentation.

Which of the following is correct?

A A Ltd is entitled to damages in the tort of deceit.

B A Ltd is entitled to have the contract set aside.

C A Ltd may request rescission of the contract or damages in lieu of rescission under the Misrepresentation Act 1967.

D A Ltd may treat the contract with B Ltd as void.

39 Which of the following is/are correct?

(i) Terms implied into a contract by a court can never override expressly agreed terms.

(ii) In some situations terms implied into a contract by a court can override expressly agreed terms.

(iii) In some situations terms implied into a contract by statute can override expressly agreed terms.

A (i) only

B (i) and (iii) only

C (ii) and (iii) only

D (i), (ii) and (iii)

40 Which of the following is incorrect?

A A condition is a term that the parties intended to be of fundamental importance.

B A warranty is a term that the parties did not intend to be of fundamental importance.

C If a condition is breached, the contract is automatically terminated.

D If a warranty is breached, the innocent party cannot treat the contract as discharged.

41 A breach of which of the following types of term never entitles the innocent party to repudiate the contract?

(i) An innominate term

(ii) A condition

(iii) A warranty

A (i) only

B (ii) only

C (iii) only

D (i) and (iii) only

42 Buyer bought some flowerpots from Seller Ltd over the Internet. Due to a mistake by the website's designer, the flowerpots were described as 12 inches in diameter whereas in reality the flowerpots are only 12cm in diameter. Buyer now wishes to return the flowerpots to Seller Ltd and get their money back on the ground of breach of contract.

Which of the following is correct?

A Buyer has a right to return the flowerpots to Seller Ltd and get their money back because the flowerpots did not correspond with the description.

B Buyer has a right to return the flowerpots to Seller Ltd and get their money back only if they can prove that Seller Ltd knew of the mis-description and had done nothing to correct it.

C Buyer has no action against Seller Ltd; their action is against the website designer.

D Buyer has no right to return the flowerpots to Seller Ltd and get their money back because the rule when buying over the Internet is 'let the buyer beware'.

43 Which of the following is/are correct?

(i) A person who signs a contract is deemed to have read it.

(ii) A person who signs a contract is bound by all its terms.

(iii) A person who has not read a contract cannot be bound by it.

A (i) only

B (ii) only

C (iii) only

D (i) and (ii) only

44 The Unfair Contract Terms Act 1977 provides that an attempt by any person to exclude or restrict their liability for damage to property resulting from negligence is:

A Void unless reasonable

B Effective only in a non-consumer transaction

C Void

D Valid

45 PQR plc contracted to hire a hotel for its annual sales conference. If the hotel becomes unavailable on the date, which of the following would frustrate the contract?

A The hotel is unusable because decorating work has overrun.

B The hotel is unusable because of a burst local authority water main.

C All the hotel's staff go on strike.

D The hotel owner realises that he under-quoted the price to PQR plc.

46 Which of the following statements relating to remedies in the law of contract is incorrect?

A The remedy of damages for breach of contract is available as of right.

B The remedy of specific performance for breach of contract is available as of right.

C An order of injunction is given at the discretion of the court.

D An order of rescission is given at the discretion of the court.

47 Which of the following statements about remedies for breach of contract is/are correct?

(i) The measure of unliquidated damages is to put the innocent party in the same position that they would have been in had the contract been properly performed.

(ii) Remoteness of loss is not relevant where a claimant is bringing an action for the price.

(iii) A claimant cannot recover unliquidated damages in respect of losses over and above those arising naturally from the breach.

A (i) only

B (i) and (ii) only

C (ii) and (iii) only

D (i), (ii) and (iii)

48 Which of the following contracts might be specifically enforceable?

(i) Propdev Ltd has contracted to sell an office building to Quentin but it has changed its mind and no longer wishes to sell it.

(ii) Susan has contracted to buy a new car of a type readily available but the garage is now refusing to honour the contract.

(iii) Spicer has contracted to perform at a gig organised by Tee plc, but Spicer has withdrawn as he wishes to go to Madrid with his wife on that date.

A (i) only

B (ii) only

C (i) and (iii) only

D (i), (ii) and (iii)

49 Which of the following is/are incorrect?

(i) Employees may be able to bring an action for unfair dismissal.

(ii) Independent contractors may be able to bring an action for unfair dismissal.

(iii) Both employees and independent contractors may be able to bring an action for wrongful dismissal.

A (i) only

B (ii) only

C (ii) and (iii) only

D (i) and (iii) only

50 **Z plc carries on business using both employees and independent contractors. It is important for Z plc to be able to distinguish between its employees and independent contractors for a number of reasons.**

Which of the following is incorrect?

A Employees have a right to statutory sick pay but this does not apply to independent contractors.

B Z plc must deduct income tax and national insurance contributions from the wages paid to its employees, but not from the amount paid to independent contractors.

C Both employees and independent contractors can enforce contractual rights against Z plc.

D Both employees and independent contractors would rank as preferential creditors in respect of unpaid wages, if Z plc went into liquidation.

51 **Which of the following is incorrect?**

A An employer is obliged to provide all employees with a reference.

B An employer must allow health and safety representatives reasonable paid time off work to perform their functions.

C Employees are entitled to a safe working environment.

D Employees are entitled to paid leave.

52 **Which of the following is/are incorrect?**

(i) An employer always has a duty to provide work for their employees.

(ii) Part-time employees cannot bring an action for unfair dismissal.

(iii) An employer must provide smoking facilities for employees who smoke.

A (i) only

B (iii) only

C (i) and (iii) only

D (i), (ii) and (iii)

53 **An employer must allow an employee time off work:**

A For trade union duties

B To attend an interview for another job

C To attend a course of training

D To attend the funeral of a close relative

54 Harry has been employed by Kay Ltd for 16 years. His contract of employment states that if either Kay Ltd or Harry wishes to terminate the contract, each party must give the statutory minimum period of notice.

Which of the following is correct?

A Both Harry and Kay Ltd are entitled to 12 weeks' notice.

B Harry is entitled to 12 weeks' notice but Kay Ltd is entitled to only 1 week's notice.

C Both Harry and Kay Ltd are entitled to 1 month's notice.

D Both Harry and Kay Ltd are entitled to 1 week's notice.

55 Which one of the following reasons cannot justify the dismissal of an employee?

A The employee's misconduct

B The employee's incompetence

C The employee joins a trade union

D The employee is unable to do the job without contravening a statute

56 A Health and Safety Executive inspector has wide powers that may be used against an employer who contravenes health and safety requirements. Which of the following Is available to the inspector?

(i) A criminal prosecution

(ii) A prohibition notice

(iii) An improvement notice

A (i) only

B (ii) only

C (iii) only

D (i), (ii) and (iii)

57 Which of the following is correct?

A The partners in a company jointly own the company's assets.

B The shareholders of a company jointly own the company's assets.

C The directors of a company jointly own the company's assets.

D Debenture holders of a company jointly own the company's assets.

58 Which of the following is/are correct in relation to a private company limited by shares?

(i) The company must have at least one director.

(ii) The company must have an authorised capital of at least £50,000.

(iii) The Memorandum of Association must state that it is a private company.

A (i) only

B (ii) only

C (i) and (iii) only

D (i), (ii) and (iii)

59 Which of the following documents must be submitted to register a company limited by shares?

(i) Memorandum of Association

(ii) A statutory declaration of compliance

(iii) A balance sheet

A (i) only

B (ii) only

C (i) and (ii) only

D (i), (ii) and (iii)

60 A public company cannot commence trading until it has received a certificate from the Registrar of Companies confirming:

A That the nominal value of the company's allotted share capital is not less than £50,000

B That the paid-up value of the company's allotted share capital is not less than £50,000

C That it has allotted at least 50,000 shares

D That it has allotted all its authorised share capital

61 Which of the following is incorrect?

A The last words in the registered name of a public limited company must be 'public limited company'.

B The last word in the registered name of a private company limited by shares must be 'limited'.

C The last word in the name of a partnership governed by the Partnership Act 1890 must be 'partnership'.

D A company may choose to trade under a name other than its registered name.

62 In relation to a company's Articles of Association, which of the following is incorrect?

A The Articles of Association set down the internal regulations of a company.

B Promoters may or may not submit their own Articles of Association when submitting the forms necessary to form a company limited by shares.

C The Articles of Association form a contract between the members and the company and the members amongst themselves.

D The Articles of Association may changed at any time by ordinary resolution.

63 Charlie is a shareholder, a director and the company secretary of SDC Ltd. Which one of the following provisions of the company's Articles of Association is enforceable by Charlie?

A Every share shall carry one vote.

B Charlie shall be a director for life.

C Charlie shall be entitled to be paid 10% more than any other director.

D Charlie shall be the company secretary for life.

64 In order to dismiss a director, under section 303 of the Companies Act 1985, the company must pass:

A A special resolution with special notice

B An ordinary resolution with special notice

C An extraordinary resolution with special notice

D An elective resolution with special notice

65 What majority is necessary to pass a special resolution?

A Just 50% of the votes that are cast

B A simple majority of the votes that are cast

C Just 75% of the votes that are cast

D More than 75% of the votes that are cast

66 Section 376 of the Companies Act 1985 allows members holding a minimum percentage of the paid-up voting rights to compel the inclusion of a resolution on the agenda of a forthcoming annual general meeting. That percentage is:

A 5%

B 10%

C 50%

D 75%

67 ABC plc has issued shares on terms that they will be bought back by the company five years after the date of issue. What are the shares called?

A Ordinary shares

B Preference shares

C Redeemable shares

D Deferred shares

68 Which of the following issues of shares is in breach of directors' fiduciary duties?

A The shares are being issued for cash to finance expansion of the company's business.

B The shares are being issued for non-cash consideration.

C The shares are being issued to secure the passing of a resolution that the existing members will not pass.

D The shares are being issued to employees under an employee share scheme.

69 HIJ plc is proposing to purchase some of its own shares.

Which of the following is incorrect?

A HIJ plc must have authority to purchase its own shares in its Articles of Association.

B If the purchase is a market purchase, the shareholders of HIJ plc must give authority by ordinary resolution.

C If the purchase is an off-market purchase, the shareholders of HIJ plc must give authority by special resolution.

D The purchase must be sanctioned by the court.

70 Which of the following is paid first where a company is in liquidation?

A Debenture holders secured by fixed charge

B Preference shareholders

C Employees who are owed wages of £800

D Debenture holders secured by floating charge

71 Delia is to become a director of DEF Ltd with a service contract for a fixed period. Which of the following is correct?

A The contract must be approved by the shareholders if the fixed period exceeds one year.

B The contract must be approved by the shareholders if the fixed period exceeds two years.

C The contract must be approved by the shareholders if the fixed period exceeds three years.

D The contract must be approved by the shareholders if the fixed period exceeds five years.

72 Kerry has acted in breach of her fiduciary duty as a director of Kay Ltd. If the breach does not amount to a fraud on the minority, which of the following is correct?

A The shareholders may not relieve Kerry from liability.

B The shareholders may relieve Kerry from liability by ordinary resolution.

C The company's articles of association may relieve Kerry from liability.

D The board of directors may relieve Kerry from liability by board resolution.

73 The liquidator of FGH Ltd has successfully brought proceedings against Freda, one of the directors, for fraudulent trading under section 213 of the Insolvency Act 1986. Which of the following may the court do?

(i) Order Freda to make a contribution to the company's assets.

(ii) Impose a fine on Freda.

(iii) Disqualify Freda from being a director for up to 15 years.

A (i) and (iii) only

B (ii) and (iii) only

C (i) only

D (i), (ii) and (iii)

74 Which of the following is incorrect?

A A managing director is appointed by the board if the Articles permit.

B A managing director is an agent of the board.

C A managing director is an agent of the company.

D Companies are not required to have a managing director.

75 Which of the following statements in relation to the company secretary is correct?

A A company secretary of a private company must be qualified.

B A company secretary of a public company must be qualified.

C A sole director of a company can also act as its company secretary.

D A company secretary must be appointed by the members in general meeting.

Section 4

ANSWERS TO MOCK ASSESSMENT

1 A

Defending your work against accusations demonstrates accountability.

2 B

The fundamental principle of integrity requires an accountant to be straightforward and honest in all professional and business relationships.

3 C

The rules-based approach sets out rules covering all foreseeable situations. This encourages a consistent application of the rules. However, it is inflexible and members may be inclined to follow the letter of the rules rather than their spirit.

4 A

Reviewing the regulatory activities of the professional accountancy bodies in relation to their members is one of the roles of the Professional Oversight Board for Accountancy.

5 D

The framework-based approach to ethics sets out general principles that members should apply to arrive at their own answer to an ethical question. It does not attempt to set out rules covering all eventualities.

6 B

The Financial Reporting Council is the United Kingdom's independent regulator for corporate reporting and governance. The Auditing Practices Board reviews the regulatory activities of the professional accountancy bodies in relation to their members. The Auditing Practices Board establishes auditing standards and issues guidance on their application. The Accounting Standards Board issues accounting standards.

7 A

Courtesy is one of the personal qualities that members of the accountancy profession need, but it is not one of the *Seven Principles of Public Life.*

8 C

The fundamental principle of professional behaviour requires a professional accountant to comply with relevant laws and regulations and avoid any action that discredits the profession.

9 D

The concept of being able to be trusted by others and being able to deliver what has been agreed when it has been agreed, is a description of the virtue of reliability.

10 D

Selflessness is one of the *Seven Principles of Public Life*. However, it is not one of the personal qualities and virtues specifically sought by CIMA.

11 C

A code of ethics tells employees what kind of behaviour is expected of them and encourages a consistent approach to ethical issues. It does not eliminate the need for legislation but, if complied with, it might minimise the need.

12 D

Linda risks passing on inaccurate information as the sales figure is not supported by other evidence. This creates an integrity issue.

13 A

Undertaking a review of accounting policies is a legitimate exercise. However, if the review is being made with the clear intention of misleading others, you should seek guidance from your professional body. If an intention to mislead is unclear, then B would be a better answer.

14 C

Promoting shares in a listed entity when that entity is a financial statement audit client is an example of an advocacy threat.

15 A

Social responsibility refers to how an organisation manages its relationships with its stakeholders, not just with its shareholders.

16 A

Rotating senior assurance team personnel is an example of an engagement-specific safeguard.

17 B

The law must always be obeyed, even if it is conflict with your *Code of Ethics*.

18 D

Ethics and governance are interrelated, so option B is incorrect. Ethics and social responsibility are both discretionary, so option C is incorrect. Codes of ethics must be compatible with legislation, rather than legislation being designed around codes of ethics, so option A is incorrect.

19 A

The Combined Code applies to all listed companies. However, the City Group for Smaller Companies (CISCO) has identified areas of the Combined Code that may prove difficult for smaller companies to implement. CISCO has suggested appropriate alternatives for smaller companies. If a small company complies with the CISCO alternatives, it is treated as complying with all the provisions of the Combined Code that it could reasonably be expected to implement.

20 D

A two-tier board comprises a management board to carry out the policy and management, and a supervisory board, which may include, for example, employee representation.

21 C

The Combined Code recommends that the roles of chairman and chief executive should be kept separate.

22 A

The Cadbury Committee recommended that executive directors should not be offered service contracts exceeding three years. The Greenbury Committee recommended that the notice period should not exceed one year.

23 C

Board structures in the United States are generally unitary in structure.

24 D

Although good governance may reduce the need for legislation, it is unlikely to eliminate it entirely. Governance is essentially voluntary rather than mandatory, so legislation may remain necessary in order to force companies to comply with best practice.

25 D

The Sarbanes-Oxley Act introduced all of these measures.

26 B

The Crown Court deals only with criminal cases. The County Court deals with civil cases. The Court of Appeal and House of Lords deal with both civil and criminal cases.

27 D

Equity prevails in a conflict between equity and the common law. Acts of Parliament and European Union regulations override both equity and common law.

28 D

If you were to rank the options in order of superiority you should come up with the following:

1. European Union regulation – this follows the rule that European Union law overrides all forms of English law.
2. Statutory instrument (a form of English delegated legislation) – this follows the principle that all forms of legislation prevail over case law.
3. *Ratio decidendi* (literally: the reason for the decision – in law referring to the rule(s) of law that led the judge to decide the case in the way they did).
4. *Obiter dicta* (literally: things said by the way; but in law meaning legal principles that a judge discussed in their judgment but which were not the reasons for the decision).

29 C

The European Commission proposes new legislation. The European Parliament and the Council of the European Union are the bodies that pass the new laws. The Court of Justice of the European Communities interprets the law, but does not create it.

30 C

All Bills must receive Royal Assent in order to become Acts of Parliament.

31 C

The three essential elements of the tort of negligence are duty of care (option A), breach of duty (option B) and resultant loss (option D).

32 B

This is the effect of the defence called 'contributory negligence'.

33 D

The legal systems of France, Germany and Poland all have elements that are codified. Denmark does not have a civil code.

34 B

The display in the shop window is an invitation to treat – *Fisher v Bell*. Burt offers to buy the telephone – *Pharmaceutical Society of Great Britain v Boots Cash Chemists*. S Ltd rejects Burt's offer.

35 C

The postal rule never applies to revocation. The postal rule is capable of applying to acceptance by posted letter, but it only actually applies when it is reasonable to use the post as a means of communication.

36 B

This question is testing your understanding of the rule in *Pinnel's* case and its exceptions.

Note that, in option D, early payment is 'satisfaction' under the principle of 'accord and satisfaction'.

37 C

A failure to disclose all relevant facts will only amount to misrepresentation in contracts of utmost good faith (e.g. insurance contracts).

38 A

Option B – rescission (i.e. having the contract 'set aside') is an equitable remedy, which may be refused by the court.

Option C – this is a remedy for negligent or innocent misrepresentation.

39 B

All court implied terms are 'gap-fillers', and therefore cannot override what the parties have expressly agreed. Some statutory implied terms are gap-fillers whereas others seek to assist whomever Parliament has decided is the weaker party to the bargain. They override what has been expressly agreed by the parties.

40 C

If a condition is breached, the innocent party may choose to treat the contract as repudiated. It is not automatically terminated.

41 C

Whether or not the innocent party can repudiate for breach of an innominate term depends on the effect of the breach. If the breach has serious consequences they can repudiate, but if trivial they cannot.

42 A

Where goods are sold by description, s13 Sale of Goods Act 1979 implies a condition into the contract between the seller and the buyer that the goods supplied correspond with their description.

43 A

We are not always bound by all the terms of a contract. For example, under the Unfair Terms in Consumer Contracts Regulations 1999, a consumer is not bound by unintelligible terms.

44 A

A person in business can exclude or restrict their liability for damage to property if the exclusion clause is reasonable.

45 B

A contract is not frustrated simply because it has become more difficult or expensive to perform. Therefore Options A, C and D are incorrect.

46 B

All equitable remedies (e.g. specific performance, injunction, and rescission) are given at the discretion of the court. In contrast a claimant has an entitlement to common law remedies (e.g. damages).

47 B

Option (iii) is incorrect because the second limb of the rule in *Hadley v Baxendale*, which deals with remoteness of loss, allows recovery of abnormal losses if they were within the reasonable contemplation of the parties at the time the contract was made.

Note that in an action for the price, a claimant who has performed their obligations under a contract is simply suing the other party for the price due to be paid under the terms of the contract.

48 A

Specific performance is commonly given of contracts for the sale or lease of land because, since land is unique, damages are an inadequate remedy. So option (i) is correct. Specific performance is not given of contracts for the sale of goods (except in the exceptional case of unique goods) because damages are an adequate remedy. So option (ii) is incorrect.

Option (iii) is incorrect because specific performance is never given of a contract for personal services.

49 B

Wrongful dismissal is an action for breach of contract. It is possible that employers might breach contracts with both employees and independent contractors.

50 D

Employees rank as preferential creditors, but independent contractors do not.

51 A

There is no legal obligation to provide an employee with a reference.

52 D

Option (i) – there is no general common law duty to provide work. Option (ii) – a claim for unfair dismissal is available to both full-time and part-time employees, provided they meet the qualifying conditions. Option (iii) – there is no legal requirement to provide facilities for smokers.

53 A

Employers are legally required to allow an employee time off for trade union duties. Time off for all the other options is at the discretion of the employer.

54 B

The statutory minimum period of notice that an employer must give depends on the length of employment, namely:

- 1 week where the employment has lasted 1 month but less than 2 years
- 1 week for each complete year where the employment has lasted 2 years but less than 12 years
- 12 weeks where employment has lasted 12 years.

The statutory minimum period of notice that an employee must give is 1 week, irrespective of the period of employment.

55 C

Options A, B and D are all categories of potentially fair dismissal as stated in the Employment Rights Act 1996. Dismissal in category C is automatically unfair.

56 D

These three are a complete list of the Health and Safety Executive's statutory powers against a defaulting employer.

57 A

A partnership does not have a separate legal existence therefore the partners are the owners of the company's assets. A company does have a separate legal existence therefore the company is the owner of its own assets.

58 A

The minimum authorised capital for a public company is £50,000; there is no equivalent requirement for a private company. The Memorandum of Association of a public company must state that it is a public company; there is no equivalent requirement for a private company.

59 C

Since the company is not yet in existence, it will not have a balance sheet, so option (iii) must of necessity be wrong.

60 A

In order to obtain a trading certificate, the plc must have issued shares totalling at least £50,000 in terms of nominal value and each share must be paid-up to at least ¼ of its nominal value plus the whole of any premium.

61 C

A partnership is not required to have the word 'partnership' in its name.

62 D

A special resolution is required to change the Articles of Association.

63 A

The Articles have contractual effect only as regards membership matters.

64 B

An ordinary resolution is used to dismiss a director. However, it requires special notice.

65 C

A special resolution requires a minimum of 75% of the votes that are cast.

66 A

Members holding at least 5% of the total voting rights can compel the inclusion of a resolution in the annual general meeting.

67 C

The shares are redeemable because there is a specified time at which the company will buy them back.

68 C

Shares must not be issued in order to dilute the voting powers of the existing members.

69 D

Do not confuse purchase of shares (no court involvement) with capital reduction (requiring court sanction).

70 A

The persons listed in the question will be repaid in the following order when a company is in liquidation. Debts secured by a fixed charge are repaid first. Employees owed wages of up to £800 are classed as preferential creditors and are repaid next. Then come floating charge holders and finally preference shareholders.

71 D

Directors' service contracts for fixed periods in excess of five years must be approved by an ordinary resolution of the shareholders. Note, however, that the *Cadbury Report* recommends this period should be reduced to three years in the case of listed companies.

72 B

The shareholders can approve a director's actions by means of an ordinary resolution.

73 D

Fraudulent trading is a criminal offence – contrast with wrongful trading.

74 B

A managing director is an agent of the company, not of the board.
Option D – note that the appointment of a Managing Director is not a statutory requirement.

75 B

A company secretary of a public company must be qualified, but there is no such requirement for a private company. A director can also act as a company secretary unless he is the sole director. The company secretary is usually appointed by the directors.